MBA Digest Book Series (1)

ENTREPRENEURSHIP AND INNOVATION:

Concise Explanations of Key MBA Topics and their Applications to Real-world Scenarios

By

Sa'idu Sulaiman
Director, Penmark Academy for Lifelong Learning,

Kano, Nigeria
Email: saisulaiman@yahoo.com

Copyright © 2024 by Sa'idu Sulaiman

All rights reserved. No part of this book shall be reproduced, stored in a retrieval system or transmitted in any form by any means without the prior written permission of author.

ISBN: 9798321575642

Published in 2024 by

Penmark Academy for Lifelong Learning, Kano

Printing & Distribution by Amazon KDP

Main parts of this book are also available in a paid course at:

https://www.udemy.com/course/mba-digest-course-on-entrepreneurship-and-innovation/?referralCode=FF387F4980857C87E0FE

ABOUT THE AUTHOR

Sa'idu Sulaiman is a retired Economics lecturer and former Director Quality Assurance at the Sa'adatu Rimi College of Education, Kano, Nigeria (now Sa'adatu Rimi University of Education).

He holds a bachelor's degree in Education / Economics, and a Postgraduate Diploma in Management. He obtained a Master of Business Administration degree from Bayero University, Kano, since 1997.

In 2015, he became a member of the London- based Institute for Small Business and Entrepreneurship (ISBE) after attending its 2014 conference in Manchester, UK.

He served as the Managing Editor of two academic journals and as the first Editor-in-Chief of the Kumbotso Teacher Educator journal (KUTEJ). He wrote a number of books, which cut across different academic disciplines.

He is the founder and Director of Penmark Academy for Lifelong Learning which is based in Kano, Nigeria. He offers the MBA Digest (MBAd) courses series on the popular Udemy online learning platform. He also runs a blog on personal finance and business tips at https://www.businessadvisor.com.ng/

TABLE OF CONTENTS

PREFACE i

CHAPTER ONE

INTRODUCTION 1

    What are MBA Courses and Why do they Matter to Us? 1

    The Cost of Obtaining MBA 2

    MBA Digest Courses as Alternatives to MBA Programs 4

CHAPTER TWO

AN OVERVIEW OF THE ACADEMIC DISCIPLINES AND THEIR CONTRIBUTIONS TO BUSINESS ADMINISTRATION 5

    Academic Disciplines that Contribute to Business Administration 5

CHAPTER THREE

ADVANTAGES OF OBTAINING AN MBA QUALIFICATION 8

    The Advantages of MBA Qualifications/MBA Digest Courses 8

CHAPTER FOUR

INTRODUCTION TO ENTREPRENEURSHIP AND INNOVATION 11

    Overview of Key Theories and Concepts 11

    Importance of Entrepreneurship and Innovation in the Business World. 12

CHAPTER FIVE

EFFECTUATION THEORY 15

    Principles of Effectuation Theory 15

    Applications of Effectuation Theory to Real-World Business Scenarios.. 17

CHAPTER SIX
INNOVATION DIFFUSION THEORY 21
The Process of Innovation Diffusion 21
Key Factors Influencing the Adoption of New Ideas and Technologies.. 23
How to Apply Innovation Diffusion Theory to Real-world Business Scenarios 25

CHAPTER SEVEN
ENTREPRENEURIAL OPPORTUNITY RECOGNITION THEORY
Introduction 28
Key Components of Entrepreneurial Opportunity Recognition Theory.. 29
Process of Identifying and Evaluating Entrepreneurial Opportunities 29
Strategies for Recognizing and Capitalizing on New Business Ideas 31

CHAPTER EIGHT
BUSINESS MODEL INNOVATION 35
Creating and Testing Innovative Business Models 35
The Role of Business Model Innovation in Driving Growth and Success 38
Applications of Innovative Business Models to Real-world Business Scenarios 40

CHAPTER NINE
MANAGING RISK AND UNCERTAINTY 43
What is Risk in Entrepreneurship? 43
What is Uncertainty in Entrepreneurship? 43
What is Risk Management in Entrepreneurship? 44
Assessing and Managing the Risks of Entrepreneurship 44

Strategies for Navigating Uncertainty and Ambiguity in the Business Environment 48

Application of Risk Assessment and Management to Real-world Business Scenarios 51

CHAPTER TEN
SCALING AND GROWTH 55

Key Factors in Scaling and Growth for Entrepreneurs 55

Scaling a New Venture 56

Managing the Challenges of Growth and Expansion 58

Application of Scaling Strategies and Managing Growth Challenges to Real-world Business Scenarios 61

CHAPTER ELEVEN
ENTREPRENEURIAL LEADERSHIP 64

Entrepreneurial Leadership Style 64

Characteristics of Successful Entrepreneurial Leaders 65

Developing Leadership Skills for Driving Innovation and Growth 67

Application of Entrepreneurial Leadership to Real-world Business Circumstances 69

CHAPTER TWELVE 73
ENTREPRENEURSHIP AND CORPORATE INNOVATION 73

The Relationship between Entrepreneurship and Corporate Innovation . 73

Strategies for Fostering a Culture of Innovation within Established Organizations 75

CHAPTER THIRTEEN
ENTREPRENEURSHIP AND SOCIAL IMPACT 79
The Role of Entrepreneurship in Driving Social Change 79
Opportunities for Creating Sustainable and Socially Responsible Businesses 80

CHAPTER FOURTEEN
ENTREPRENEURSHIP AND GLOBALIZATION 83
Challenges and Opportunities of Entrepreneurship in a Globalized Economy 83
Strategies for Expanding into International Markets 85

CHAPTER FIFTEEN 88
ENTREPRENEURIAL FINANCE 88
Funding Options for Entrepreneurs 88
Financial Planning and Management 90
Valuation and Exit Strategies 93

CHAPTER SIXTEEN
ARTIFICIAL INTELLIGENCE, BUSINESS, AND SOCIETY 97
AI Applications in Business 98
Ethical and Social Implications of AI 101
Strategies for Promoting Ethical AI Practices in Business Organizations 103
Future Trends and Opportunities 105

CHAPTER SEVENTEEN
BUSINESS PLAN AND APPLIED BUSINESS RESEARCH 109

Key Components of a Business Plan 109

Market Analysis and Strategy 113

Significance of Applied Business Research to Entrepreneurs 116

Data Collection and Analysis 118

Strategic Recommendations 121

APPENDIX I
GLOSSARY OF ENTREPRENUERSHIP AND INNOVATIONS TERMS 125

APPENDIX II
SAMPLE BUSINESS PLAN 133

PREFACE

In today's world, there are MBA degree programs in which students specialize in Entrepreneurship and Innovation. Examples of institutions that offer these programs include Martin Tuchman School of Management, under New Jersey Institute of Technology. Its program focuses on enabling students to identify business opportunities, create new businesses, and innovate with sustainable new technologies and business models (https://management.njit.edu/mba-innovation-and-entrepreneurship).

Another example is the Wharton Entrepreneurship and Innovation MBA specialization that seeks to provide students "with skills, analytical tools, perspectives, and experiences that prepare them for careers as autonomous entrepreneurs, family-business entrepreneurs, or entrepreneurs in corporate settings," (https://mgmt.wharton.upenn.edu/programs/mba/entrepreneurship-innovation/)

The third example is International College of Management, Sydney. The objectives of its MBA Entrepreneurship and Innovation program, are among others, to enable students make decisions to enhance business performance by drawing on integrated knowledge of core business, Innovation and Entrepreneurship disciplines with critical ethical judgement (https://www.icms.edu.au/courses/post-graduate/master-of-business-administration-innovation-and-entrepreneurship/).
Another example is IU International University of Applied Sciences. It is Germany's biggest university. Its mission is to create inclusive, global and wholly accessible education, so it offers an online MBA entrepreneurship degree program.

Finally, Harvard Business School also offers MBA entrepreneurship program that comprises a required curriculum for the first year. This curriculum requires all students to take the same course of study to enable them get broad foundation of general management concepts and skills. The elective curriculum designed for the second year, allows students choose from a range of elective courses (https://entrepreneurship.hbs.edu/programs/mba/Pages/courses.aspx)

After examining topics included in the MBA Entrepreneurship and Innovation of these institutions, I discovered some similarities and differences in them. These cannot be unconnected to the fact that the institutions consider their learning goals which also differ. The MBA digest (MBAd) book on Entrepreneurship and Innovation, I'm introducing to you will cover key topics which I tactically selected from what these institutions offer to give you diverse knowledge and skills related to Entrepreneurship and Innovation. The contents of the book are also supplemented with their real-world applications to business scenarios.

The book is essentially derived from my MBA Digest course on Entrepreneurship and Innovation where I used my knowledge and cognate experiences to review, edit and adopt AI generated contents (ChatGPT 3.5) and other sources to create the course. The course is available on Udemy at this address: https://www.udemy.com/course/mba-digest-course-on-entrepreneurship-and-innovation/?referralCode=FF387F4980857C87E0FE

My objectives of publishing the book is to enable prospective readers who could not enroll in the course do the following:

1. Explain key theories and concepts related to entrepreneurship and innovation, such as effectuation theory, innovation diffusion theory, and entrepreneurial opportunity recognition theory.

2. Analyze the principles of effectuation theory and apply them to real-world entrepreneurial decision-making scenarios.

3. Evaluate the process of innovation diffusion and identify factors that influence the adoption of new ideas and technologies in the business world.

4. Identify and assess entrepreneurial opportunities, utilizing entrepreneurial opportunity recognition theory to evaluate the feasibility and potential of new business ideas.

5. Develop innovative business models and test their effectiveness in driving growth and success for new ventures.

6. Assess and manage the risks associated with entrepreneurship, and develop strategies for navigating uncertainty and ambiguity in the business environment.

7. Design strategies for scaling a new venture and managing the challenges of growth and expansion.

8. Identify the characteristics of successful entrepreneurial leaders and develop leadership skills for driving innovation and growth in a new venture.

9. Analyze the relationship between entrepreneurship and corporate innovation, and develop strategies for fostering a culture of innovation within established organizations.

10. Explore the role of entrepreneurship in driving social impact and develop strategies for creating sustainable and socially responsible businesses.

11. Examine the challenges and opportunities of entrepreneurship in a globalized economy, and develop strategies for expanding into international markets.

12. State various sources of funding available to entrepreneurs, explain the importance of financial planning and management to entrepreneurs and take note of key considerations for valuation and exit strategies in the context of entrepreneurial ventures.

13. Describe various ways in which Artificial Intelligence is being applied in business contexts to enhance operations, improve decision-making, and drive competitive advantage, and also explain the implications of AI on business and society.

14. Apply key theories and concepts to a real-world business scenario and write a comprehensive business plan for a new venture by means of a recommended capstone project.

The book is meant for aspiring entrepreneurs intending to launch a new business, MBA students seeking for condensed and simplified course contents, and business owners wanting to increase their knowledge and skill in the areas of entrepreneurship and innovation. Managing Directors and CEOs seeking to sharpen their skillsets and employees aiming for senior management roles in private and governmental organizations will also benefit from this book.

CHANGES AND INNOVATIONS FOR ENHANCING LIFELONG LEARNING

The first Master of Business Administration (MBA) program was established at Harvard University in 1908, and since then, the degree has gained widespread popularity and recognition around the world. Today, Harvard does not only accept change and innovation in providing MBA related programs, it also initiates them.

The Division of Continuing Education (DCE) at Harvard University makes Harvard education accessible to lifelong learners from high school to retirement. It introduced a new MBA alternative called *Business Management Program: From Management to Leadership*. The program consists of highly interactive lectures, case discussions, exercises, and workshops. The program is for managers across industries and functional areas, and working professionals who are starting a business, human resource professionals, consultants, and business administrators. The DCE says, over the course of five days, participants in this program "will engage in an MBA-inspired curriculum focused on skills that drive business success. Upon completion of the program, you will earn a Certificate of Participation from the Harvard Division of Continuing Education." (Sourced from https://professional.dce.harvard.edu/blog/beyond-the-traditional-mba-exploring-alternative-mba-routes-to-business-excellence/)

The MBA Digest (MBAd) courses and book series are also MBA inspired initiatives meant to facilitate lifelong learning among people that accept change and innovation to enhance their personal and professional development. *Accept changes and innovations, join the courses and or read the books to boost your knowhow and skills.*

CHAPTER ONE

INTRODUCTION

What are MBA Courses and Why do they Matter to Us?

As we delve into the intricate world of business, governance of organizations and their resources, one vital course stands out, the Master of Business Administration course. The first MBA program was established at Harvard University in 1908, and since then, the degree has gained widespread popularity and recognition around the world.

MBA courses taught in Harvard, Wharton, Oxford University, and Bayero University from where I obtained my MBA in 1997, and, of course, in other world universities, cover a wide range of topics.

The early MBA programs focused primarily on management and leadership skills, with an emphasis on practical application and real-world problem-solving.

Over time, the curriculum has expanded to include a wide range of business disciplines, such as organizational behavior, human resource management, finance, marketing management, operations management, corporate strategy and the rest.

The research I conducted for my Postgraduate Diploma in Management course, focused on the process of developing and executing business objectives in selected textile firms in Kano State. A lay man would think that getting profit is the only objective for doing business. The research I conducted for my MBA program was an appraisal of corporate social responsibility of selected manufacturing firms in Kano State. These researches fall under corporate strategy which is a vital course in MBA programs.

From what I've said, you can see how MBA matters to us and to the organizations we establish or work for. Obtaining an MBA will turn you into a vital asset to your business, or to any business, governmental or non-governmental organization that employs you. This is because it teaches you how to manage people in organizations, how to manage humans and other resources, how to manage operations, how to market products and ideas, to name a few.

The Cost of Obtaining MBA

Highly priced goods and services often have a great value, the MBA program is not different in this regard.

The Investopia.com site reveals that MBA Degrees cost very much. It says, in 2022, the first-year budget for the Wharton MBA program was almost $119,000. This includes $85,000 for tuition, $23,000 for room and board, $7,000 for books and supplies, and $4,000 for health insurance. The site also states that an estimated cost of two-year MBA program at the University of Chicago was almost $156,000 in 2022, while an online MBA at the Eller College of Management through the University of Arizona would cost $51,525 and takes as little as 14 months to complete. https://www.investopedia.com/terms/m/mba.asp#

A 2024 article by Education Data Initiative provides the following information on the cost of MBA: https://educationdata.org/average-cost-of-a-masters-degree

- The average cost of a Master's degree in Business Administration is $56,850.
- The average cost of an MBA degree from 1999 to 2022 was $52,763.
- The cost of an MBA degree from Harvard Business School for a full 2-year program is $231,276.
- The cost of an MBA degree from Binghamton University is $22,620 for a 2-year program.

A 2023 article by Forbes submits that "tuition is not the only cost to consider for MBA programs. You also have to factor in administration fees, textbooks, transportation expenses and your state's typical cost of living." It explains that having a clear goal before considering an MBA is essential to a strong return in investment (ROI) as earning an MBA is an investment in yourself. A direct "way of calculating the ROI of an MBA would be by dividing your potential post-MBA salary by the total cost of your MBA, including tuition, fees, living expenses and lost wages during your studies," the articles further explains. https://www.forbes.com/advisor/education/business-and-marketing/mba-cost/

No wonder, the Glassdoor website, reports that the total pay range for an MBA holder in USA in 2023 was $89,000 - $161,000 per year(https://www.glassdoor.com/Salaries/mba-salary-SRCH_KO0,3.htm)

MBA Digest Courses as Alternatives to MBA Programs

If you cannot obtain an MBA degree due to time or financial constraints, why not settle for what I call MBA Digest courses? Half a loaf is better than none.

MBA Digest courses are concise courses tactically distilled from vital MBA courses offered in world universities, and supplemented with real-world applications to business scenarios. Each course in the series has distinct objectives, contents and real-world applications to business scenarios, so prospective learners interested in any course or a number of courses, can pay for and get enrolled in them.

With these courses you can also acquire some of the essential abilities, skills and mindsets possessed by MBA graduates and take your personal and professional development to the next levels.

CHAPTER TWO

AN OVERVIEW OF THE ACADEMIC DISCIPLINES AND THEIR CONTRIBUTIONS TO BUSINESS ADMINISTRATION

Business administration draws its content from various academic disciplines, each of which contributes unique perspectives and knowledge that are essential for understanding and managing organizations and business operations.

Academic Disciplines that Contribute to Business Administration

Here's an overview of some academic disciplines and their contributions to business administration:

Various academic disciplines contribute to the multidisciplinary nature of business administration, providing a holistic understanding of the complex and dynamic business environment. These include:

1. Economics: Economics provides the foundational understanding of how individuals, businesses, and societies allocate scarce resources to meet unlimited wants. It offers insights into market behavior, pricing, supply and demand, and the impact of economic policies on business operations.

2. Psychology: Psychology contributes to business administration by providing insights into individual and group behavior, motivation, decision-making, and leadership. Understanding

human behavior is crucial for managing employees, customers, and stakeholders effectively.

3. Sociology: Sociology offers perspectives on organizational behavior, group dynamics, social structures, and the impact of societal trends on business practices. It helps in understanding organizational culture, diversity, and social responsibility.

4. Accounting: Accounting provides the language of business, offering tools and techniques for financial reporting, analysis, and decision-making. It helps in understanding financial statements, budgeting, cost analysis, and performance measurement.

5. Marketing: Marketing contributes to business administration by focusing on customer behavior, market research, product development, branding, advertising, and sales strategies. It provides insights into creating and delivering value to customers.

6. Operations Management: This discipline focuses on the design, management, and improvement of processes that create and deliver products and services. It includes areas such as supply chain management, quality control, and process optimization.

7. Finance: Finance offers knowledge about investment, capital markets, risk management, and financial decision-making. It provides tools for managing capital, evaluating investment opportunities, and understanding financial markets.

8. Strategy: Drawing from fields such as strategic management and organizational theory, strategy focuses on long-term planning, competitive advantage, industry analysis, and decision-making at the organizational level.

These academic disciplines, among others, contribute to the multidisciplinary nature of business administration, providing a holistic understanding of the complex and dynamic business environment. Integrating insights from these diverse fields is essential for effective decision-making and problem-solving in the business world.

The early MBA programs focused primarily on management and leadership skills, with an emphasis on practical application and real-world problem-solving. Over time, the curriculum has expanded to include a wide range of business disciplines, such as finance, marketing, operations, and strategy.

The evolution of the MBA has been shaped by various factors, including changes in the global business environment, advancements in technology, and shifts in educational philosophy. As a result, modern MBA programs are designed to prepare graduates for the complexities and challenges of today's business world, with a focus on innovation, sustainability, and ethical leadership.

CHAPTER THREE

ADVANTAGES OF OBTAINING AN MBA QUALIFICATION

This chapter covers the numerous advantages of obtaining an MBA qualification. Many of these advantages can also be obtained by people that enroll and master the MBA Digest courses I am offering on Udemy or read my books in the MBA digest courses series.

The Advantages of MBA Qualifications/MBA Digest Courses

The advantages of obtaining an MBA qualification, and perhaps of mastering my MBA digest courses/books include the following:

1. Enhanced Career Opportunities:

One of the primary advantages of obtaining an MBA qualification is the access to enhanced career opportunities. Many employers actively seek out candidates with MBA degrees for leadership and management positions. The specialized knowledge and skills acquired during an MBA program can make individuals more competitive in the job market and open doors to higher-level roles within organizations.

2. Expanded Professional Network:

Another key benefit of pursuing an MBA is the opportunity to expand one's professional network. MBA programs often bring together a diverse group of students from various backgrounds and industries. This networking opportunity can lead to valuable connections with peers, faculty, and industry professionals, which can be instrumental in career advancement, business partnerships, and entrepreneurial endeavors.

3. Developed Leadership Skills:

An MBA program is designed to cultivate leadership and management skills in its students. Through coursework, case studies, and group projects, individuals can develop critical thinking, strategic decision-making, and effective communication skills. These leadership competencies are highly sought after in the business world and can significantly contribute to professional success.

4. Specialized Knowledge and Expertise:

MBA programs offer the opportunity to gain specialized knowledge and expertise in various areas of business, such as finance, marketing, operations, and entrepreneurship. This comprehensive understanding of business functions (this) equips individuals with the ability to analyze complex business challenges and develop innovative solutions, making them valuable assets to organizations seeking strategic thinkers.

5. Entrepreneurial Opportunities:

For individuals aspiring to start their own businesses, an MBA qualification can provide a solid foundation for entrepreneurial success. MBA programs often offer coursework focused on entrepreneurship, business planning, and venture capital, providing aspiring entrepreneurs with the knowledge and skills necessary to launch and manage successful ventures.

6. Global Perspective and Cultural Awareness:

In an increasingly globalized business environment, an MBA program can offer exposure to international business practices, cross-cultural management, and global market dynamics. This global perspective and cultural awareness are essential for professionals operating in diverse and interconnected markets, making an MBA qualification particularly valuable for those pursuing international career opportunities.

Conclusion

The advantages of obtaining an MBA qualification are multifaceted. They include career advancement, professional development, networking opportunities, and the acquisition of specialized skills and knowledge. As the business landscape continues to evolve, an MBA remains a valuable asset for individuals seeking to excel in their careers and make a meaningful impact in the global business arena.

CHAPTER FOUR

INTRODUCTION TO ENTREPRENEURSHIP AND INNOVATION

This chapter will cover definitions of entrepreneurship and innovation and their relationships. It will also provide you with some key points highlighting the importance of entrepreneurship and innovation in the business world.

Overview of Key Theories and Concepts

Entrepreneurship and innovation are two closely intertwined concepts that play a crucial role in driving economic growth, creating new opportunities, and fostering creativity and change in the business world. In this introductory session, we will explore the fundamental principles of entrepreneurship and innovation, and understand their significance in today's dynamic and competitive business environment.

1. Definition of Entrepreneurship:

Entrepreneurship can be defined as the process of identifying, creating, and pursuing opportunities to start new ventures or bring innovative ideas to market. Entrepreneurs are individuals who take calculated risks, think creatively, and demonstrate a strong sense of initiative and perseverance in pursuing their business goals.

2. Definition of Innovation:

Innovation refers to the process of developing new products, services, processes, or business models that create value for customers and differentiate a company from its competitors. Innovation can take many forms, including incremental improvements to existing products or services, as well as disruptive innovations that transform entire industries.

3. Relationship between Entrepreneurship and Innovation:

Entrepreneurship and innovation are closely interconnected, as entrepreneurs often drive innovation by identifying new opportunities, taking risks, and introducing novel ideas to the market. Innovation, in turn, fuels entrepreneurship by creating new business opportunities and enabling entrepreneurs to develop competitive advantages in the marketplace.

Importance of Entrepreneurship and Innovation in the Business World

Entrepreneurship and innovation play a crucial role in the business world by driving economic growth, creating job opportunities, and fostering technological advancements. Here are some key points highlighting the importance of entrepreneurship and innovation:

1. Economic Growth: Entrepreneurship and innovation are key drivers of economic growth as they lead to the creation of new products, services, and industries. Entrepreneurs identify gaps in the market and develop innovative solutions that meet the needs of consumers, thereby stimulating economic activity and increasing productivity.

2. Job Creation: Entrepreneurs are often the primary job creators in the economy. By starting new businesses and expanding existing ones, entrepreneurs generate employment opportunities, reduce

unemployment rates, and contribute to the overall prosperity of society.

3. Technological Advancements: Innovation is at the heart of entrepreneurship, leading to the development of new technologies, processes, and products that enhance efficiency, quality, and competitiveness. Entrepreneurs drive technological advancements by investing in research and development, experimenting with new ideas, and pushing the boundaries of what is possible.

4. Competition and Market Dynamics: Entrepreneurship fosters competition in the marketplace, encouraging businesses to constantly innovate and improve their offerings to stay ahead. This (Market Dynamics) dynamic environment benefits consumers by providing them with a wider range of choices, better quality products, and competitive prices.

5. Wealth Creation: Successful entrepreneurs have the potential to create significant wealth for themselves, their employees, and their investors. This wealth creation has a ripple effect on the economy, leading to increased consumer spending, investment in other businesses, and overall economic prosperity.

6. Social Impact: Entrepreneurship and innovation can have a positive social impact by addressing societal challenges, such as poverty, healthcare, education, and environmental sustainability. Social entrepreneurs, in particular, focus on creating businesses that have a dual purpose of generating profits and making a positive impact on society.

7. Adaptability and Resilience: Entrepreneurs are known for their ability to adapt to changing market conditions, overcome obstacles, and persevere in the face of challenges. This resilience is

essential in today's rapidly evolving business landscape, where agility and innovation are key to survival and success.

In conclusion, entrepreneurship and innovation are essential components of a thriving business ecosystem. They drive economic growth, create employment opportunities, foster technological advancements, and have a positive impact on society. Encouraging and supporting entrepreneurship and innovation is crucial for businesses, economies, and societies to thrive in an ever-changing world.

CHAPTER FIVE

EFFECTUATION THEORY

This chapter will explain the key principles of effectuation theory and how they can be applied to real-world business scenarios.

Principles of Effectuation Theory

In ordinary English, to effectuate something means to create it or to cause it to happen. Effectuation theory is about creating entrepreneurship opportunities. Developed by Saras Sarasvathy, effectuation theory focuses on how successful entrepreneurs approach decision-making and opportunity creation. Sarasvathy is *an American entrepreneurship professor* and recipient of the 2022 Global Award for Entrepreneurship Research. Unlike traditional approaches to entrepreneurship that emphasize predicting and controlling the future, her effectuation theory argues that entrepreneurs should embrace uncertainty, use their existing resources, and focus on creating opportunities rather than simply exploiting them. The following are the key principles of effectuation theory:

1. Bird-in-Hand Principle:

The bird-in-hand principle suggests that entrepreneurs should start with their existing resources, such as their skills, knowledge, and network, and use them to create opportunities. By focusing on what they have rather than what they lack, entrepreneurs can take practical steps towards realizing their goals and building a successful venture.

2. Affordable Loss Principle:

The affordable loss principle encourages entrepreneurs to take calculated risks by focusing on what they are willing to lose rather than what they stand to gain. By setting limits on their potential losses and being prepared for different outcomes, entrepreneurs can make decisions that are less risky and more manageable, allowing them to explore new opportunities with greater confidence.

3. Crazy Quilt Principle:

The crazy quilt principle emphasizes the importance of building partnerships and alliances with others to co-create value and share resources. Entrepreneurs should leverage the diverse skills and perspectives of their network to access new opportunities, gain valuable insights, and overcome challenges that they may not be able to address on their own.

4. Lemonade Principle:

The lemonade principle encourages entrepreneurs to be flexible and adaptable in response to unexpected events or setbacks. Instead of viewing obstacles as insurmountable barriers, entrepreneurs should see them as opportunities to pivot, innovate, and turn lemons into lemonade by finding creative solutions and alternative pathways to success.

5. Pilot-in-the-Plane Principle:

The pilot-in-the-plane principle emphasizes the role of the entrepreneur as an active agent who shapes and influences the future through his actions and decisions. Entrepreneurs should (be) take a proactive approach to decision-making, continuously learning and adapting to changing circumstances, and steering their venture towards success through their vision, determination, and resourcefulness.

In conclusion, effectuation theory offers a valuable perspective on entrepreneurship that challenges traditional notions of planning and prediction. By focusing on leveraging existing resources, taking calculated risks, building partnerships, embracing flexibility, and maintaining a proactive mindset, entrepreneurs can adopt a more effective and innovative approach to creating and growing successful ventures.

Applications of Effectuation Theory to Real-World Business Scenarios

Effectuation theory has been widely applied in the field of entrepreneurship to understand how successful entrepreneurs think and act in uncertain and complex environments. By embracing the principles of effectuation, entrepreneurs can navigate ambiguity, capitalize on emerging opportunities, and build resilient and adaptive ventures that thrive in today's fast-paced and competitive business landscape.

Effectuation theory can be applied to real-world business scenarios in various ways, helping entrepreneurs and business leaders navigate uncertainty, make strategic decisions, and create opportunities for growth and innovation. Here are some examples of how effectuation theory can be applied in practical business situations:

1. Leveraging Existing Resources:

In a startup scenario where resources are limited, entrepreneurs can apply the bird-in-hand principle of effectuation by leveraging their existing skills, knowledge, and network to create value. For example, a software developer with expertise in a specific programming language can start a consulting business or develop a new software product based on their skills and experience, rather than waiting for external funding or resources.

A Prophetic saying of Muhammad, peace be upon him, relates that a poor man from among the Ansar came to the Prophet (saw) and begged from him. He said, "Do you have anything in your house?" The poor man replied: "Yes, a blanket, part of which we cover ourselves with and part we spread beneath us, and a bowl from which we drink water." The poor man was then instructed to bring the items and they were sold for two dirhams. The Prophet (saw) instructed the man to buy an axe (a capital asset for a firewood selling business) with one dirham, and use the remaining money to feed his family. After fifteen days, the poor man returned to the Prophet (saw) with ten dirhams he realized from his business. This event, which happened over 1400 years, bear a resemblance to the bird-in-hand principle of effectuation. It is recorded in Hadith No. 2198 in the book *Sunan Ibn Majah,* Chapter 14, narrated by Anas bin Malik.

2. Taking Calculated Risks:

In a product development context, entrepreneurs can apply the affordable loss principle of effectuation by setting limits on their potential losses and experimenting with new ideas in a controlled manner. For instance, a food entrepreneur looking to launch a new line of healthy snacks can test different recipes and packaging options with a small group of customers before investing in large-scale production, minimizing the risk of failure and optimizing their product offering.

3. Building Partnerships and Alliances:

In a competitive market where collaboration is key to success, entrepreneurs can apply the crazy quilt principle of effectuation by forming strategic partnerships and alliances with complementary businesses or industry stakeholders. For example, a technology startup developing a new mobile app can partner with a marketing agency to promote their product, leverage their expertise in customer acquisition, and reach a wider audience through targeted campaigns and partnerships.

4. Embracing Flexibility and Adaptability:

In a rapidly changing industry where market trends and consumer preferences evolve quickly, entrepreneurs can apply the lemonade principle of effectuation by being flexible and adaptable in response to unexpected challenges or disruptions. For instance, a retail business facing a downturn in foot traffic due to a shift towards online shopping can pivot to e-commerce, offer personalized shopping experiences, and explore new revenue streams such as subscription services or virtual events to stay competitive and meet changing customer needs.

5. Maintaining a Proactive Mindset:

In a growth-oriented business environment where innovation is critical to staying ahead of the competition, entrepreneurs can apply the pilot-in-the-plane principle of effectuation by taking a proactive approach to decision-making and continuously learning and adapting to new opportunities. For example, a manufacturing company exploring new markets can invest in research and development, collaborate with industry experts, and test new product prototypes to identify emerging trends, address customer needs, and drive long-term growth and profitability.

By applying the principles of effectuation theory in real-world business scenarios, entrepreneurs can develop a strategic mindset, make informed decisions, and create value through innovative and resourceful approaches that lead to sustainable business success and competitive advantage.

CHAPTER SIX

INNOVATION DIFFUSION THEORY

This chapter examines the process of innovation diffusion, key factors influencing the adoption of new ideas and technologies, lastly, how to apply innovation diffusion theory to real-world business scenarios.

The word diffusion means spread, dissemination or dispersal. Innovation diffusion theory was created by Everett Rogers, a communication scholar at the University of New Mexico. He popularized it in his book *Diffusion of Innovations* published in 1962. The process of innovation diffusion refers to how new ideas, technologies, products, or practices spread and are adopted within a society or organization.

The Process of Innovation Diffusion

The process of innovation diffusion follows a series of stages that individuals or groups typically go through when encountering and deciding whether to adopt an innovation. These stages are:

1. Awareness: The first stage of innovation diffusion is when individuals become aware of the existence of the innovation. This can happen through various channels such as advertising, media coverage, word-of-mouth, or personal experience. Awareness is crucial as it introduces the innovation to potential adopters and sparks their interest.

2. Interest: Once individuals are aware of the innovation, they develop an interest in learning more about it. This stage involves seeking information, researching the innovation, and understanding its potential benefits and applications. Interest is essential for moving individuals from awareness to consideration.

3. Evaluation: In the evaluation stage, individuals assess the innovation based on its relevance to their needs, compatibility with existing practices, potential advantages, and disadvantages. This stage involves weighing the costs, risks, and benefits of adopting the innovation to determine its value proposition.

4. Trial: The trial stage involves experimenting with the innovation on a small scale. This could involve a pilot project, test run, or limited implementation to evaluate its performance, gather feedback, and assess its impact in a controlled environment. Trial helps individuals gain firsthand experience with the innovation before committing to full adoption.

5. Adoption: If the trial phase is successful and individuals are convinced of the innovation's benefits, they may decide to adopt it on a larger scale. Adoption involves integrating the innovation into regular practices, processes, or systems to realize its full potential and benefits.

6. Implementation: The implementation stage involves deploying the innovation across the organization or society. This includes training, support, and monitoring to ensure a smooth transition and effective integration of the innovation into daily operations.

7. Confirmation: After the innovation has been implemented, individuals evaluate its performance and outcomes to confirm whether it has met their expectations and goals. This stage involves

collecting feedback, measuring results, and making adjustments to optimize the innovation's effectiveness.

Key Factors Influencing the Adoption of New Ideas and Technologies

The adoption of new ideas and technologies is influenced by a variety of factors that can impact the rate and extent of their acceptance within a society or organization. Understanding these factors is crucial for innovators, businesses, and policymakers to effectively promote and facilitate the adoption of innovations.

Some key factors that influence the adoption of new ideas and technologies include:

1. Relative Advantage: The perceived superiority of the new idea or technology compared to existing alternatives is a significant factor influencing adoption. If individuals or organizations believe that the innovation offers clear advantages in terms of efficiency, effectiveness, cost savings, or other benefits, they are more likely to adopt it.

2. Compatibility: The compatibility of the new idea or technology with existing values, beliefs, practices, and infrastructures is important for adoption. Innovations that align with current norms and ways of working are more likely to be accepted and integrated into existing systems.

3. Complexity: The complexity of the new idea or technology can impact adoption rates. Innovations that are easy to understand, use, and implement are more likely to be adopted quickly, while those that are overly complicated or require significant changes may face resistance.

4. Trialability: The ability to test the new idea or technology on a small scale before full adoption can facilitate its acceptance. Offering opportunities for individuals or organizations to experiment with the innovation and see its benefits firsthand can help build confidence and reduce perceived risks.

5. Observability: The visibility of the new idea or technology and its results to others can influence adoption decisions. If individuals can see the positive outcomes and benefits of the innovation demonstrated by others, it can create social proof and encourage adoption.

6. Perceived Risk: The perceived risks associated with adopting a new idea or technology, such as financial investment, time commitment, or potential negative consequences, can impact adoption decisions. Minimizing perceived risks through clear communication, support, and guarantees can help increase adoption rates.

7. Social Influence: Social factors, such as peer pressure, social norms, and cultural values, can play a significant role in the adoption of new ideas and technologies. Individuals are often influenced by the opinions and behaviors of their social networks, making social influence a powerful factor in adoption decisions.

8. Regulatory Environment: The regulatory environment, including laws, policies, and standards, can also shape the adoption of new ideas and technologies. Regulations that support or inhibit innovation can impact the willingness of individuals or organizations to adopt new solutions.

By considering these factors and addressing potential barriers to adoption, innovators, businesses, and policymakers can enhance the likelihood of successful adoption and integration of new ideas and technologies into society or organizations.

How to Apply Innovation Diffusion Theory to Real-world Business Scenarios

Innovation Diffusion Theory can be applied to real-world business scenarios to understand and predict how new ideas or technologies spread within organizations and industries. Here are some examples of how this theory can be applied:

1. Product Launch Strategy

When a company is launching a new product or service, they can use Innovation Diffusion Theory to identify early adopters, influencers, and *laggards* within their target market. A laggard is an individual or organization that is slow to adopt new technologies, ideas, or trends compared to others in the market.

By targeting early adopters first, the company can create momentum and generate positive word-of-mouth that can help drive adoption among the broader market.

Example: Apple's product launches, such as the iPhone or iPad, often target early adopters and influencers who help create buzz and excitement around the new product before it reaches mainstream adoption. Mainstream adoption occurs when a product or service gains widespread acceptance and usage among the general population or target market.

2. Technology Adoption in Organizations

Businesses can use Innovation Diffusion Theory to understand how new technologies are adopted within their organization. By identifying factors that influence adoption, such as relative advantage, compatibility, and complexity, companies can develop strategies to facilitate the adoption process and address potential barriers.

Example: A manufacturing company implementing a new Industry 4.0 technology like IoT sensors on the production line can use Innovation Diffusion Theory to ensure that employees understand the benefits of the technology, see how it aligns with their existing processes, and receive adequate training to use it effectively.

3. Marketing Campaigns

Marketers can apply Innovation Diffusion Theory to design campaigns that target different segments of the market based on their adoption behavior. By tailoring messages and incentives to early adopters, early majority, and late majority, companies can accelerate the adoption of their products or services.

Example: A software company launching a new project management tool can use targeted marketing campaigns to appeal to early adopters who value innovation and cutting-edge features, while later targeting the early majority with case studies and testimonials showcasing the tool's benefits.

4. Change Management

Organizations undergoing significant changes, such as restructuring, mergers, or digital transformations, can use Innovation Diffusion Theory to manage resistance and facilitate the adoption of new processes or systems. By understanding the concerns and motivations of different employee groups, companies can develop communication strategies and training programs to support successful adoption.

Example: A retail company transitioning to an omnichannel sales model can use Innovation Diffusion Theory to identify early adopters among store managers who can champion the change, influence their peers, and help drive adoption of new technologies

CHAPTER SEVEN

ENTREPRENEURIAL OPPORTUNITY RECOGNITION THEORY

Introduction

The Entrepreneurial Opportunity Recognition Theory was originally proposed by Scott Shane of University of Maryland and S. Venkataraman of the same university, in their paper titled "Entrepreneurship as a Field of Research: Encouraging Dialogue and Debate." (The Academy of Management Review, Vol. 25, No. 1 (Jan., 2000), pp. 217-226 https://www.jstor.org/stable/259271)

Alexander Ardichvili from University of Illinois, Richard Cardozo from University of Minnesota, and Sourav Ray from John Molson School of Business, Concordia University, also published a journal article titled "A theory of entrepreneurial opportunity identification and development" in which they propose a theory of the opportunity identification process". The theory identifies entrepreneur's personality traits, social networks, and prior knowledge as antecedents of entrepreneurial alertness to business opportunities. (*Journal of Business Venturing*, Volume 18, Issue 1, 1 January 2003, Pages 105-123. https://www.sciencedirect.com/science/article/abs/pii/S0883902601000684)

Entrepreneurial Opportunity Recognition Theory focuses on how entrepreneurs identify and seize opportunities in the market. This theory suggests that successful entrepreneurs possess the ability to spot opportunities that others may miss and have the skills to turn these opportunities into profitable business ventures.

Key Components of Entrepreneurial Opportunity Recognition Theory

Key components of Entrepreneurial Opportunity Recognition Theory include cognitive factors, social factors, environmental factors, and prior knowledge and experience.

Cognitive factors refer to the mental processes that entrepreneurs use to identify opportunities, such as creativity, problem-solving, and pattern recognition.

Social factors emphasize the importance of networks and relationships in providing valuable information and insights for opportunity recognition.

Environmental factors, such as economic conditions and technological advancements, can also influence opportunity identification.

Additionally, prior knowledge and experience play a significant role in helping entrepreneurs recognize opportunities based on their past experiences and expertise.

The Process of Identifying and Evaluating Entrepreneurial Opportunities

Identification and Evaluation of Entrepreneurial Opportunities is a critical process in entrepreneurship that involves recognizing potential business opportunities and assessing their viability for creating successful ventures. This process requires entrepreneurs to be proactive, creative, and strategic in identifying opportunities and evaluating their potential for success. Being proactive involves taking initiative, anticipating challenges, and acting in advance to prevent problems or capitalize on opportunities. Being strategic involves setting long-term goals, making informed decisions, and aligning actions with the overall vision of the business.

1. Identification of Opportunities: Entrepreneurs need to actively seek out opportunities in the market by staying informed about industry trends, consumer needs, technological advancements, and regulatory changes. Opportunities can arise from gaps in the market, emerging trends, changing customer preferences, or advancements in technology. Entrepreneurs must be observant, open-minded, and willing to *think outside the box* to identify potential opportunities. To think outside the box is to approach problems or situations in unconventional or innovative ways to find creative solutions.

2. Evaluation of Opportunities: Once opportunities are identified, entrepreneurs need to evaluate them to determine their feasibility and potential for success. This involves conducting market research, analyzing competition, assessing customer demand, and evaluating the financial viability of the opportunity. Entrepreneurs should consider factors such as market size, growth potential, *competitive landscape*, and resource requirements when evaluating opportunities. The competitive landscape is the overall market environment in which businesses operate, including competitors, industry trends, and market dynamics.

3. Risk Assessment: Entrepreneurs should also assess the risks associated with pursuing a particular opportunity. This includes evaluating potential challenges, uncertainties, and obstacles that may impact the success of the venture. By conducting a thorough

risk assessment, entrepreneurs can make informed decisions about whether to pursue or abandon an opportunity.

4. Feasibility Analysis: Feasibility analysis involves assessing the viability and potential success of a business idea or project based on factors such as market demand, resources, and technical feasibility. Entrepreneurs should conduct a feasibility analysis to determine if the opportunity aligns with their skills, resources, and goals. This analysis helps entrepreneurs assess whether they have the capabilities and capacity to pursue the opportunity successfully. It also helps in identifying potential challenges and developing strategies to overcome them.

5. Opportunity Prioritization: Not all opportunities are equal, and entrepreneurs may need to prioritize and focus on the most promising ones. By evaluating and comparing different opportunities based on their potential for success, entrepreneurs can allocate their time, energy, and resources effectively to maximize their chances of building a successful venture.

The process of identifying and evaluating entrepreneurial opportunities is essential for entrepreneurs to create successful businesses. By being proactive, conducting thorough research, assessing risks, and prioritizing opportunities, entrepreneurs can increase their chances of identifying viable opportunities and turning them into successful ventures.

Strategies for Recognizing and Capitalizing on New Business Ideas

Recognizing and capitalizing on new business ideas is a crucial aspect of entrepreneurship that can lead to the creation of successful ventures. Here are some strategies that entrepreneurs can use to effectively identify and capitalize on new business ideas:

1. Identify Market Needs: One of the key strategies for recognizing new business ideas is to identify unmet market needs or gaps. Conducting market research, analyzing consumer trends, and understanding *customer pain points* can help entrepreneurs pinpoint opportunities for innovative solutions. Customer pain points are specific problems, challenges, or frustrations that customers experience, which businesses aim to address and solve through their products or services. By addressing specific market needs, entrepreneurs can create value for customers and differentiate their offerings from competitors.

2. Stay Curious and Open-Minded: Being curious and open-minded can help entrepreneurs discover new business ideas in unexpected places. By exploring diverse industries, attending networking events, and engaging in conversations with people from different backgrounds, entrepreneurs can gain fresh perspectives and insights that may inspire new business ideas. Staying curious and open-minded allows entrepreneurs to think creatively and identify opportunities that others may overlook.

3. Utilize Technology and Innovation: Leveraging technology and innovation can be a powerful strategy for recognizing and capitalizing on new business ideas. Keeping abreast of technological advancements, industry trends, and *disruptive innovations* can help entrepreneurs identify opportunities to leverage technology to create innovative products or services. Disruptive innovations are groundbreaking advancements or technologies that create new markets, disrupt existing industries, and fundamentally change the way businesses operate. By embracing

innovation, entrepreneurs can stay ahead of the curve and capitalize on emerging trends in the market.

4. Collaborate and Network: Collaborating with industry experts, mentors, and other entrepreneurs can provide valuable insights and opportunities for generating new business ideas. Networking with like-minded individuals, attending industry events, and participating in entrepreneurial communities can help entrepreneurs expand their knowledge base, gain new perspectives, and uncover potential opportunities for collaboration or partnership. Building a strong network can also lead to valuable feedback and support for refining and *validating new business idea.* Validating a new business idea means confirming or authenticating it.

5. Test and Validate Ideas: Before fully committing resources to a new business idea, it is important to test and validate its feasibility. Conducting market research, running pilot tests, gathering feedback from potential customers, and analyzing data can help entrepreneurs assess the viability and market potential of a new business idea. By testing and validating ideas early on, entrepreneurs can reduce risks and make informed decisions about pursuing or refining a business concept.

6. Embrace Continuous Learning: Continuous learning and self-improvement are essential for entrepreneurs to stay competitive and innovative. By seeking out learning opportunities, staying updated on industry developments, and acquiring new skills, entrepreneurs can expand their knowledge base and increase their ability to recognize and capitalize on new business ideas. Embracing a growth mindset and a willingness to learn from failures can also help entrepreneurs adapt to changing market conditions and seize opportunities for growth.

By employing these strategies, entrepreneurs can enhance their ability to recognize and capitalize on new business ideas. By staying informed, staying curious, leveraging technology, collaborating with others, testing ideas, and embracing continuous learning, entrepreneurs can increase their chances of identifying innovative opportunities and building successful ventures in today's dynamic business environment.

CHAPTER EIGHT

BUSINESS MODEL INNOVATION

This chapter focuses on creating and testing innovative business models; the role of business model innovation in driving growth and success; and applications of innovative business models to real-world business scenarios.

Creating and Testing Innovative Business Models

Creating and testing innovative business models is a crucial aspect of entrepreneurship that involves developing new approaches to generating revenue, delivering value to customers, and sustaining competitive advantage. Here are some key steps and considerations for creating and testing innovative business models:

1. Identifying Market Needs: The first step in creating an innovative business model is to identify unmet market needs, emerging trends, and changing customer preferences. By understanding the *pain points* and desires of customers, entrepreneurs can develop business models that address specific challenges or offer unique *value propositions*. The pain points of customers refer to the specific problems, challenges, or frustrations they have, which businesses aim to address and solve through their products or services. A value proposition is a statement that communicates the unique benefits and value that a product or service offers to customers.

2. Design Thinking: Design thinking is a human-centered approach to innovation that focuses on understanding the needs

of users, generating creative solutions, and prototyping ideas. By applying design thinking principles, entrepreneurs can develop customer-centric business models that are user-friendly, intuitive, and effective in meeting customer needs. Prototyping ideas involves creating tangible representations or mock-ups of concepts to visualize, test, and refine new product or service ideas.

3. Value Proposition: A value proposition is a statement that communicates the unique benefits and value that a product or service offers to customers, distinguishing it from your competitors produce. A strong value proposition is essential for creating an innovative business model. Entrepreneurs should clearly articulate the unique benefits and advantages of their products or services to customers. By defining a compelling value proposition, entrepreneurs can differentiate their offerings in the market and attract target customers.

4. Revenue Model: Developing a sustainable revenue model is critical for the long-term success of a business. A revenue model outlines how a business generates income through sales, subscriptions, advertising, or other revenue streams. Entrepreneurs should explore different revenue streams, pricing strategies, and monetization models to generate consistent income and support business growth. Testing and refining the revenue model is essential to ensure its viability and profitability.

5. Prototyping and Testing: Before fully implementing a new business model, entrepreneurs should create prototypes, conduct pilot tests, and gather feedback from customers and stakeholders. By testing the feasibility and effectiveness of the business model in a controlled environment, (with tests) entrepreneurs can identify

potential challenges, refine the model, and make informed decisions about its implementation.

6. Iterative Approach: Creating and testing innovative business models often requires an *iterative approach*. An iterative approach involves making incremental changes and improvements to the core elements of a business model based on feedback and market insights. Entrepreneurs should be willing to experiment, adapt to feedback, and make adjustments to the business model based on real-world testing and validation. By iterating on the business model, entrepreneurs can improve its effectiveness, scalability, and sustainability over time.

7. Market Validation: Market validation is the process of confirming the demand, viability, and potential success of a product or service through testing, research, and feedback from customers. It is an essential step in testing innovative business models. Entrepreneurs should validate the demand for their products or services, assess market dynamics, and evaluate the competitive landscape to ensure the viability and potential success of the business model. Market validation helps entrepreneurs make data-driven decisions and mitigate risks associated with launching a new venture.

Creating and testing innovative business models require a combination of creativity, strategic thinking, customer focus, and iterative testing. By following these steps and considerations, entrepreneurs can develop innovative business models that address market needs, deliver unique value, and drive sustainable growth in today's dynamic business environment.

The Role of Business Model Innovation in Driving Growth and Success

Business model innovation plays a crucial role in driving growth and success for organizations across industries. By reimagining how businesses create, deliver, and capture value, companies can differentiate themselves, adapt to changing market conditions, and capitalize on new opportunities.

Here are some key points highlighting the importance of business model innovation in driving growth and success:

1. Competitive Advantage: Business model innovation enables organizations to create a unique competitive advantage by offering *differentiated products or services*, optimizing operational efficiency, and delivering superior customer value. Differentiated products or services offer unique features, benefits, or qualities that set them apart from competitors in the market. By developing innovative business models, companies can stand out in the market, attract customers, and outperform competitors.

2. Market Relevance: In today's rapidly evolving business landscape, staying relevant and meeting changing customer needs is essential for long-term success. Business model innovation allows companies to adapt to market trends, technological advancements, and shifting consumer preferences. By continuously innovating their business models, organizations can *stay ahead of the curve* and remain competitive in dynamic markets. Staying ahead of the curve means anticipating trends, innovations, and market shifts to maintain a competitive edge and lead the industry.

3. Revenue Growth: Business model innovation can drive revenue growth by identifying new revenue streams, optimizing existing ones, and expanding market reach. By exploring innovative pricing strategies, partnership opportunities, and *monetization models*, companies can unlock new sources of income and maximize profitability. Monetization models outline how businesses generate revenue from their products or services, including pricing strategies, subscription models, and advertising methods. Business model innovation is a key driver of revenue diversification and sustainable growth.

4. Operational Efficiency: Innovating business models can improve operational efficiency, streamline processes, and reduce costs. By rethinking how resources are allocated, workflows are structured, and value is delivered, organizations can enhance productivity, optimize resource utilization, and drive performance improvements. Business model innovation is essential for driving operational excellence and achieving sustainable growth.

5. Customer Value: Business model innovation focuses on creating and delivering unique value to customers. By understanding customer needs, preferences, and pain points, organizations can develop business models that address specific challenges, offer personalized solutions, and enhance customer experience. By prioritizing customer value creation, companies can build strong relationships, foster loyalty, and drive business success.

6. Adaptability and Resilience: Business model innovation enhances an organization's adaptability and resilience (i.e. flexibility) in the face of uncertainty and disruption. By being proactive, agile, and open to change, companies can respond to market shifts, industry disruptions, and competitive threats effectively. Business model innovation enables organizations to

anticipate challenges, identify opportunities, and pivot their strategies to navigate complex business environments.

7. Innovation Culture: Embracing business model innovation fosters a culture of creativity, experimentation, and continuous improvement within organizations. By encouraging employees to think innovatively, challenge the status quo, and explore new possibilities, companies can drive a culture of innovation that fuels growth and success. Business model innovation is a catalyst for organizational transformation and sustainable innovation.

Business model innovation is a powerful driver of growth and success for organizations seeking to thrive in today's competitive and dynamic business landscape. By embracing innovation, adapting to change, and focusing on delivering value to customers, companies can unlock new opportunities, drive revenue growth, and build a sustainable competitive advantage. Business model innovation is a strategic imperative for organizations looking to drive growth, enhance competitiveness, and achieve long-term success in an ever-changing business environment.

Applications of Innovative Business Models to Real-world Business Scenarios

Creating innovative business models is a critical process that can be applied to real-world business circumstances to drive growth, competitiveness, and sustainability. By developing and validating new approaches to value creation, delivery, and capture, organizations can stay ahead of the curve, adapt to market changes, and capitalize on emerging opportunities.

Here are some examples of how creating and testing innovative business models can be applied in real-world business scenarios:

1. Subscription-Based Model: Many companies are shifting from traditional one-time sales to subscription-based business models, offering customers ongoing access to products or services in exchange for a recurring fee. For example, Netflix revolutionized the entertainment industry by introducing a subscription-based streaming service, allowing customers to access a vast library of content for a monthly subscription fee. By continuously testing and refining their subscription model, Netflix has attracted a large customer base, increased customer retention, and achieved sustainable revenue growth.

2. Peer-to-Peer Sharing Economy: The rise of the sharing economy has enabled individuals to monetize their assets by sharing them with others through online platforms. Companies like Airbnb and Uber have transformed the hospitality and transportation industries by connecting hosts with guests and drivers with passengers, respectively. By testing and iterating on their peer-to-peer business models, these companies have created new revenue streams, disrupted traditional industries, and provided innovative solutions to consumers' needs.

3. Freemium Model: The term *freemium* comes from a combination of the words "free" and "premium". The freemium business model offers a basic version of a product or service for free, with the option to upgrade to a premium version with additional features or functionalities for a fee. For example, software companies like Dropbox and Spotify offer free versions of their products with limited capabilities, enticing users to upgrade to premium plans for enhanced features. By testing different pricing tiers, features, and value propositions, these companies have successfully monetized their user base, increased customer engagement, and driven revenue growth.

4. Direct-to-Consumer (DTC) Model: Direct-to-consumer brands bypass traditional retail channels and sell their products directly to customers through online platforms, cutting out intermediaries and offering a personalized shopping experience. Companies like Warby Parker and Casper disrupted the eyewear and mattress industries, respectively, by selling their products directly to consumers at competitive prices. By testing their online sales channels, marketing strategies, and customer engagement tactics, these DTC brands have built strong brand loyalty, gained market share, and achieved rapid growth.

5. Platform Business Model: Platform businesses create digital ecosystems that connect multiple stakeholders, such as buyers, sellers, and service providers, facilitating transactions, interactions, and value exchange. Examples include Amazon, eBay, and Airbnb, which act as intermediaries between users, enabling them to buy, sell, or rent goods and services. By continuously testing and optimizing their platform features, user experience, and monetization strategies, these companies have built scalable business models, expanded their reach, and generated substantial revenue. Scalable business models are models which are designed to grow and expand efficiently without compromising quality or increasing costs exponentially as the business expands.

In each of these real-world examples, creating business models have been instrumental in driving business success, fostering innovation, and capturing market opportunities. By experimenting with different approaches, gathering feedback from customers, and adapting to changing market dynamics, organizations can develop sustainable business models that deliver unique value, drive growth, and ensure long-term viability in today's competitive business landscape.

CHAPTER NINE

MANAGING RISK AND UNCERTAINTY

Managing risk and uncertainty is a fundamental aspect of entrepreneurship, as startups and small businesses often operate in dynamic and unpredictable environments. In order to succeed and thrive in the competitive business landscape, entrepreneurs must effectively navigate the challenges posed by risk and uncertainty. This requires a strategic approach to identifying, assessing, and mitigating potential risks, as well as the ability to adapt to changing circumstances and seize opportunities in the face of uncertainty.

What is Risk in Entrepreneurship?

Risk in entrepreneurship refers to the potential for loss or failure associated with business decisions and actions. Entrepreneurs face a variety of risks, including financial risks, market risks, operational risks, and strategic risks. Financial risks, for example, may involve investment decisions, cash flow management, or funding challenges. Market risks relate to factors such as changing customer preferences, competitive pressures, or economic fluctuations. Operational risks encompass issues like supply chain disruptions, technology failures, or regulatory compliance. Full explanation of these types of risk will come in another lecture.

What is Uncertainty in Entrepreneurship?

Uncertainty in entrepreneurship refers to the lack of predictability or clarity about future outcomes. Entrepreneurs often operate in environments characterized by ambiguity, volatility, and rapid change, making it difficult to forecast market trends, customer behavior, or competitive dynamics. Uncertainty can stem (result) from factors such as technological advancements, regulatory changes, global events, or shifts in consumer preferences. Entrepreneurs must navigate this uncertainty by staying agile, adaptive, and responsive to emerging opportunities and threats.

What is Risk Management in Entrepreneurship?

Risk management in entrepreneurship involves the systematic process of identifying, assessing, and mitigating risks to minimize their impact on the business. Effective risk management strategies enable entrepreneurs to make informed decisions, protect their assets, and enhance their chances of success. This may involve implementing risk mitigation measures, developing contingency plans, diversifying business activities, or securing insurance coverage. By proactively managing risks, entrepreneurs can enhance their resilience, seize opportunities for growth, and sustain long-term competitiveness in the market.

Managing risk and uncertainty is a critical aspect of entrepreneurship that requires a proactive and strategic approach. By understanding the nature of risk and uncertainty, implementing effective risk management strategies, and staying agile in the face of uncertainty, entrepreneurs can navigate challenges, capitalize on opportunities, and drive sustainable growth and success in their ventures.

Assessing and Managing the Risks of Entrepreneurship

Assessing and managing the risks of entrepreneurship is a fundamental aspect of building a successful and sustainable business. Entrepreneurs encounter a myriad of risks that can impact their operations, financial stability, and overall *growth trajectory*. Growth trajectory refers to the path and rate at which a business expands over time. It involves analyzing factors such as revenue growth, market share, customer acquisition, and profitability to understand the trajectory of a company's growth and potential future performance.

By proactively identifying potential risks, assessing their potential impact, and implementing effective risk management strategies, entrepreneurs can enhance their ability to navigate challenges and seize opportunities. Here are some examples of common risks faced by entrepreneurs and strategies for managing them:

1. Financial Risk:
Financial risk is a primary concern for entrepreneurs, as insufficient funding or cash flow issues can impede business growth. To manage financial risk effectively, entrepreneurs can:
- Conduct comprehensive financial planning and forecasting to anticipate *cash flow* requirements. Cash flow represents the movement of money in and out of a business, indicating its liquidity and ability to meet financial obligations. Positive cash flow means that a company is generating more cash than it is spending, while negative cash flow may signal financial challenges
- Explore diverse funding sources, such as *venture capital, angel investors,* or *crowdfunding.*
  Venture capital is a type of private equity investment provided to early-stage, high-potential startups with the expectation of significant returns. Venture capitalists typically take equity stakes in companies and provide funding, expertise, and support to help them grow and succeed. Angel investors are affluent individuals who provide financial backing to startups in exchange for equity ownership. They often invest in early-stage companies and

play a crucial role in supporting entrepreneurship by offering capital, mentorship, and industry connections. Crowdfunding is a method of raising capital from a large number of individuals, typically through online platforms, to finance a business venture or project.

- Implement stringent financial management practices, including budgeting, cost control, and monitoring key financial metrics.

2. Market Risk:

Market risk encompasses uncertainties related to changing consumer preferences, competitive dynamics, and market trends. To mitigate market risk, entrepreneurs can:
- Conduct market research to understand customer needs, preferences, and behavior.
- Monitor industry trends, competitor activities, and market developments to identify potential threats and opportunities.
- Develop a flexible marketing strategy that can adapt to evolving market conditions and consumer demands.

3. Operational Risk:

Operational risk involves challenges associated with day-to-day business operations, such as *supply chain disruptions*, technology failures, or compliance issues. Supply chain disruptions occur when there are interruptions or challenges in the flow of goods, materials, or information within a company's supply chain. To manage operational risk effectively, entrepreneurs can:
- Establish robust operational processes and procedures to ensure efficiency and consistency.

- Implement risk management protocols to identify and address potential operational vulnerabilities.
- Cultivate strong relationships with suppliers, partners, and stakeholders to mitigate supply chain disruptions and operational challenges.

4. Legal and Regulatory Risk:

Legal and regulatory risk pertains to compliance issues, lawsuits, or changes in legislation that can impact business operations. To mitigate legal and regulatory risk, entrepreneurs can:

- Stay abreast of relevant laws, regulations, and industry standards that affect their business.
- Seek guidance from legal advisors to ensure compliance with regulations and mitigate legal exposure.
- Implement internal controls and policies to proactively address legal and regulatory requirements and minimize potential liabilities.

5. Strategic Risk:

Strategic risk involves decisions related to business growth, *market positioning*, and *product development* that can influence the long-term success of the venture. Market positioning involves defining how a company's products or services are perceived by customers relative to competitors. It encompasses strategies to differentiate a brand, target specific market segments, and create a unique value proposition to stand out in the marketplace. Product development is the process of creating, designing, and bringing new products or services to market. It involves research, ideation, prototyping, testing, and refinement to ensure that the product meets customer needs and aligns with the company's objectives. To manage strategic risk effectively, entrepreneurs can:

- Conduct a comprehensive *SWOT analysis* to evaluate internal strengths, weaknesses, external opportunities, and threats. SWOT analysis is a strategic planning tool used to assess a company's Strengths, Weaknesses, Opportunities, and Threats.
- Develop a clear and adaptive business strategy that aligns with market trends and customer needs.
- Continuously evaluate and adjust strategic plans based on performance metrics, market feedback, and emerging trends to stay competitive and innovative.

In conclusion, assessing and managing the risks of entrepreneurship is a critical component of building a resilient and successful business. By proactively identifying and addressing potential risks, implementing robust risk management strategies, and maintaining agility in the face of uncertainties, entrepreneurs can enhance their ability to navigate challenges, capitalize on opportunities, and drive sustainable growth in their ventures.

Strategies for Navigating Uncertainty and Ambiguity in the Business Environment

Navigating uncertainty and ambiguity in the business environment is a crucial skill for entrepreneurs to develop, especially in today's rapidly changing and unpredictable market landscape. Market landscape refers to the overall structure, dynamics, and trends of a specific industry or market segment. By adopting strategic approaches and leveraging innovative tactics, entrepreneurs can effectively manage uncertainties and capitalize on opportunities. Leveraging innovative tactics means using creative and unconventional approaches to solve problems, differentiate a business, and gain a competitive edge in the market.

Here are some strategies for navigating uncertainty and ambiguity in the business environment, along with examples:

1. Embrace Flexibility and Adaptability:

One key strategy for navigating uncertainty is to remain flexible and adaptable in response to changing circumstances. This involves being open to new ideas, adjusting strategies as needed, and pivoting quickly when necessary. For example, during the COVID-19 pandemic, many businesses shifted their operations online, adapted their products or services to meet changing customer needs, and implemented remote work policies to ensure business continuity.

2. Foster a Culture of Innovation:

Encouraging a culture of innovation within the organization can help entrepreneurs navigate uncertainty by fostering creativity, experimentation, and a willingness to take calculated risks. By empowering employees to think outside the box and explore new ideas, businesses can stay ahead of the curve and adapt to changing market dynamics. For instance, companies like Google and Amazon are known for their innovative cultures that prioritize experimentation and continuous improvement.

3. Build Strategic Partnerships:

Collaborating with strategic partners, suppliers, and stakeholders can help entrepreneurs navigate uncertainty by leveraging complementary strengths, sharing resources, and expanding market reach. By forming strategic alliances, businesses can access new markets, technologies, and expertise to mitigate risks and capitalize on growth opportunities. For example, Apple's partnership with Nike to create the Apple Watch Nike+ combined technology and fitness expertise to target health-conscious consumers.

4. Invest in Technology and Data Analytics:

Utilizing technology and data analytics can provide businesses with valuable insights to navigate uncertainty by identifying trends, predicting market shifts, and making informed decisions. Market shifts refer to changes in consumer behavior, industry trends, technology advancements, or competitive dynamics that impact the business environment. By leveraging data-driven strategies, entrepreneurs can optimize operations, personalize customer experiences, and stay competitive in a rapidly evolving marketplace. For instance, companies like Netflix use data analytics to recommend personalized content to users based on their viewing habits and preferences.

5. Develop Contingency Plans:

Creating contingency plans and risk management strategies can help entrepreneurs navigate uncertainty by preparing for potential challenges and disruptions. By identifying potential risks, developing mitigation strategies, and establishing clear protocols for crisis response, businesses can minimize the impact of unforeseen events and maintain business continuity. For example, airlines have contingency plans in place to address flight cancellations, weather disruptions, or other unforeseen events to minimize passenger inconvenience and ensure safety.

6. Stay Customer-Centric:

Customer-centricity is a business approach that prioritizes delivering exceptional value and experiences to customers by understanding their needs, preferences, and feedback. Maintaining a customer-centric focus can help entrepreneurs navigate uncertainty by prioritizing customer needs, preferences, and feedback. By listening to customers, gathering insights, and adapting products or services based on their feedback, businesses can build loyalty, drive innovation, and stay relevant in a competitive market. For example, companies like Zappos and Amazon have built their success on a customer-centric approach that prioritizes exceptional service and personalized experiences.

Navigating uncertainty and ambiguity in the business environment requires a combination of strategic foresight, adaptability, innovation, and customer-centricity. By embracing flexibility, fostering innovation, building strategic partnerships, leveraging technology and data analytics, developing contingency plans, and prioritizing customer needs, entrepreneurs can effectively manage uncertainties, seize opportunities, and drive sustainable growth in their businesses.

Application of Risk Assessment and Management to Real-world Business Scenarios

Assessment and management of risks are essential components of effective business operations, as they help entrepreneurs identify potential threats, plan for contingencies, and make informed decisions to mitigate risks. By applying risk assessment and management strategies to real-world business scenarios, entrepreneurs can enhance their ability to navigate uncertainties, protect their assets, and drive sustainable growth.

Here are some examples of how the assessment and management of risks can be applied to real-world business scenarios:

1. Cybersecurity Risks: Scenario: A small e-commerce business experiences a data breach, resulting in the exposure of customer information and financial data. Application of Risk Assessment and Management:

- Conduct a cybersecurity risk assessment to identify vulnerabilities, assess potential threats, and evaluate the impact of a data breach on the business.
- Implement cybersecurity measures such as encryption, firewalls, and regular security audits to protect customer data and mitigate the risk of cyberattacks.
- Develop a data breach response plan outlining steps to contain the breach, notify affected customers, and comply with data protection regulations to minimize reputational damage and financial losses.

2. Supply Chain Risks: Scenario: A manufacturing company faces disruptions in its supply chain due to a natural disaster impacting key suppliers. Application of Risk Assessment and Management:

- Conduct a supply chain risk assessment to identify critical suppliers, assess potential risks, and develop contingency plans for supply chain disruptions.

- Diversify suppliers, establish alternative sourcing options, and maintain buffer inventory to reduce reliance on a single supplier and mitigate the impact of disruptions.
- Monitor supply chain performance, communicate proactively with suppliers, and implement risk-sharing agreements to build resilience and ensure continuity of operations during unforeseen events.

3. Financial Risks: Scenario: A startup company experiences cash flow challenges due to unexpected expenses and a decline in sales revenue. Application of Risk Assessment and Management:

- Conduct a financial risk assessment to evaluate liquidity, profitability, and financial stability, identify potential risks, and develop strategies to manage cash flow effectively.
- Implement financial controls, budgeting processes, and cash flow forecasting to monitor expenses, optimize revenue streams, and maintain financial health.
- Explore financing options such as lines of credit, loans, or equity investments to address short-term cash flow gaps and support business growth while minimizing financial risks.

4. Market Risks: Scenario: A retail business faces declining sales due to changing consumer preferences, competitive pressures, and economic uncertainties. Application of Risk Assessment and Management:

- Conduct a market risk assessment to analyze market trends, competitive landscape, and consumer behavior, identify potential risks, and develop strategies to adapt to changing market conditions.

- Implement market research, customer surveys, and trend analysis to anticipate shifts in consumer preferences, identify emerging opportunities, and differentiate products or services to stay competitive.
- Diversify product offerings, target new customer segments, and explore new distribution channels to expand market reach, mitigate risks of revenue decline, and drive sustainable growth in a dynamic market environment.

The application of risk assessment and management to real-world business scenarios is critical for entrepreneurs to proactively identify, evaluate, and mitigate risks that can impact business operations, financial performance, and long-term sustainability. By applying risk assessment tools, developing risk management strategies, and implementing proactive measures to address cybersecurity risks, supply chain disruptions, financial challenges, and market uncertainties, entrepreneurs can enhance their resilience, protect their assets, and capitalize on opportunities to drive success in their ventures.

CHAPTER TEN

SCALING AND GROWTH

Scaling refers to the process of increasing the size and scope of a business, while growth involves the expansion of a business in terms of revenue, customer base, market reach, and profitability. Scaling and growth are crucial aspects of entrepreneurship that determine the success and sustainability of a business. Entrepreneurs often strive to achieve sustainable growth by scaling their businesses effectively.

Key Factors in Scaling and Growth for Entrepreneurs

One key factor in scaling and growth for entrepreneurs is the ability to identify and capitalize on opportunities for expansion. This may involve entering new markets, offering new products or services, or targeting new customer segments. Customer segments are distinct groups of consumers with similar characteristics, needs, and behaviors. By continuously innovating and adapting to changing market conditions, entrepreneurs can drive growth and scale their businesses to new heights.

Another important aspect of scaling and growth is the ability to manage resources effectively. As a business expands, entrepreneurs must ensure that they have the necessary infrastructure, talent, and financial resources to support growth. This may involve investing in technology, hiring skilled employees, and optimizing operational processes to accommodate increased demand.

Furthermore, strategic partnerships and collaborations can play a significant role in scaling and growth for entrepreneurs. By forming alliances with other businesses, leveraging networks, and seeking mentorship from industry experts, entrepreneurs can access new opportunities for growth and scale their businesses more efficiently.

In addition, a strong focus on customer acquisition and retention is essential for sustainable growth. By delivering exceptional products or services, providing excellent customer service, and building strong relationships with customers, entrepreneurs can drive growth through repeat business, referrals, and positive word-of-mouth marketing.

Overall, scaling and growth in entrepreneurship require a combination of strategic planning, resource management, innovation, and customer-centric focus. By effectively scaling their businesses and driving sustainable growth, entrepreneurs can achieve long-term success and create value for their stakeholders.

Scaling a new venture is a critical phase in the growth and development of a business. It involves expanding the operations, customer base, and market reach of the venture to achieve sustainable growth and profitability.

Scaling a New Venture

To successfully scale a new venture, entrepreneurs can implement the following strategies:

1. Develop a Scalable Business Model: Ensure that the business model is designed to accommodate growth and expansion. This may involve streamlining operations, automating processes, and

creating systems that can easily scale as the business grows. Streamlining operation means optimizing and simplifying the workflows and procedures within a business to improve efficiency, reduce costs, and enhance productivity.

2. Focus on Product-Market Fit: Product-Market Fit refers to the alignment between a company's product or service offering and the needs and preferences of its target market. Continuously assess and refine the product or service offerings to meet the needs and preferences of the target market. By understanding customer feedback and market trends, entrepreneurs can tailor their offerings to achieve a strong product-market fit.

3. Build a Strong Team: As the business scales, it is essential to hire talented employees who can support growth and drive innovation. Building a strong team with diverse skills and expertise is crucial for scaling a new venture successfully.

4. Invest in Technology: Leveraging technology can help streamline operations, improve efficiency, and enhance the customer experience. Investing in scalable technology solutions can enable the business to handle increased demand and expand its capabilities.

5. Expand Marketing and Sales Efforts: Increase marketing and sales efforts to reach a broader audience and attract new customers. Implement targeted marketing campaigns, explore new sales channels, and build strategic partnerships to drive growth and expand market reach.

6. Secure Funding: Scaling a new venture often requires additional capital to support expansion initiatives. Entrepreneurs can seek funding from investors, venture capitalists, or through

crowdfunding to finance growth opportunities and fuel the scaling process. Crowdfunding means raising capital from a large number of individuals, usually through online platforms, to finance a business venture or project.

7. Monitor Key Performance Indicators (KPIs): Establish key performance indicators to track the progress and success of the scaling efforts. Metrics that need monitoring include customer acquisition cost and customer lifetime value. Customer acquisition involves the process of attracting and converting potential customers into paying clients. Customer lifetime value is the predicted net profit a company expects to earn from a customer throughout their entire relationship with the business. Other metrics for evaluating the effectiveness of scaling strategies are revenue growth and profitability.

8. Adapt and Iterate: Stay agile and adaptable in response to market changes and feedback from customers. Continuously *iterate* on strategies, products, and processes to optimize performance and drive sustainable growth. Iterating means making incremental changes and improvements to the core elements of these things based on feedback and market insights.

By implementing these strategies and approaches, entrepreneurs can effectively scale their new ventures, expand their market presence, and position the business for long-term success and profitability.

Managing the Challenges of Growth and Expansion

Managing the challenges of growth and expansion is a critical aspect of entrepreneurship that requires strategic planning, effective decision-making, and adaptability. As a business scales and expands, entrepreneurs may encounter various challenges that can impact the success and sustainability of the venture. To effectively manage these challenges, entrepreneurs can implement the following strategies:

1. Resource Management: One of the key challenges of growth and expansion is managing resources effectively. Entrepreneurs need to ensure that they have the necessary financial, human, and technological resources to support expansion initiatives. By optimizing resource allocation, monitoring expenses, and investing in scalable infrastructure, entrepreneurs can mitigate resource constraints and facilitate growth.

2. Operational Efficiency: As a business grows, operational complexity may increase, leading to inefficiencies and bottlenecks. Entrepreneurs should focus on *streamlining processes* and automating tasks. Streamlining processes involves optimizing and simplifying the workflows, procedures, and operations within a business to improve efficiency, reduce costs, and enhance productivity. They should also focus on implementing systems and technologies that enhance operational efficiency. By improving workflow, reducing waste, and enhancing productivity, businesses can better manage the challenges of growth and expansion.

3. Talent Acquisition and Development: Scaling a business requires a skilled and motivated workforce to support growth initiatives. Entrepreneurs should focus on recruiting top talent, providing training and development opportunities, and fostering a positive work culture to attract and retain employees. By investing in human capital, businesses can overcome challenges related to talent management and build a strong team to drive growth.

4. Market Expansion and Competition: Expanding into new markets and facing increased competition are common challenges of growth and expansion. Entrepreneurs should conduct thorough market research, identify competitive threats, and develop strategies to differentiate their offerings and capture market share. By staying informed about market trends, customer preferences, and competitor activities, businesses can navigate challenges related to market expansion and competition effectively.

5. Financial Management: Managing finances becomes more complex as a business scales and expands. Entrepreneurs should maintain financial discipline, monitor cash flow, and seek additional funding sources to support growth initiatives. By creating financial projections, setting budgets, and conducting regular financial reviews, businesses can address challenges related to financial management and ensure long-term sustainability.

6. Customer Satisfaction and Retention: As a business grows, maintaining high levels of customer satisfaction and retention becomes crucial. Entrepreneurs should prioritize customer service, gather feedback from customers, and address any issues promptly to ensure a positive customer experience. By building strong relationships with customers, businesses can overcome challenges related to customer satisfaction and retention and drive loyalty and advocacy.

7. Risk Management: With growth and expansion come increased risks and uncertainties. Entrepreneurs should conduct risk assessments, develop contingency plans, and proactively manage risks to protect the business from potential threats. By identifying and mitigating risks, businesses can navigate challenges related to growth and expansion more effectively and ensure resilience in the face of adversity.

By implementing these strategies and approaches, entrepreneurs can effectively manage the challenges of growth and expansion, drive sustainable growth, and position their businesses for long-term success and profitability. Adaptability, resilience, and strategic planning are key factors in overcoming challenges and seizing opportunities for growth and expansion in the dynamic business environment.

Application of Scaling Strategies and Managing Growth Challenges to Real-world Business Scenarios

By applying these strategies and approaches to real-world business scenarios, entrepreneurs and business leaders can effectively scale their ventures, manage the challenges of growth and expansion, and position their businesses for long-term success in competitive markets. The following examples show how entrepreneurs apply Strategies for Scaling their business or manage the challenges of growth and expansion to real-world business scenarios.

1. Strategies for Scaling a New Venture:

a) Focus on Product-Market Fit: Companies like Uber focused on understanding customer needs and preferences to tailor their services accordingly. By continuously refining their offerings based on market feedback, they were able to scale their business successfully.

b) Build a Strong Team: Companies such as Google prioritize hiring top talent to drive innovation and growth. By assembling a team of skilled professionals with diverse backgrounds, they can leverage different perspectives and expertise to propel the business forward.

c) Invest in Technology: Tech companies like Amazon invest heavily in technology to enhance customer experience and streamline operations. By leveraging advanced technologies like artificial intelligence and data analytics, they can optimize processes and scale their operations efficiently.

d) Expand Marketing and Sales Efforts: Companies like Coca-Cola focus on expanding their market reach through targeted marketing campaigns and strategic partnerships. By increasing brand visibility and engaging with customers effectively, they can drive sales and grow their customer base.

e) Secure Funding: Startups like SpaceX secure funding from investors and venture capitalists to support growth initiatives. By raising capital through funding rounds, they can invest in research and development, expand their operations, and scale their business effectively.

2. *Managing the Challenges of Growth and Expansion:*

a) Resource Management: Companies like Apple face challenges in managing resources effectively during periods of rapid growth. By optimizing production processes, streamlining supply chain operations, and investing in infrastructure, they can ensure efficient resource allocation and sustainable growth.

b) Operational Efficiency: Companies such as Walmart focus on improving operational efficiency to meet growing demand and maintain profitability. By implementing lean practices, automation technologies, and supply chain optimization strategies, they can enhance productivity and reduce costs.

c) Talent Acquisition and Development: Companies like Microsoft prioritize talent acquisition and development to support growth initiatives. By attracting top talent, providing training and development opportunities, and fostering a positive work culture, they can build a strong team to drive innovation and success.

d) Market Expansion and Competition: Companies like Nike expand into new markets globally and face competition from both established players and emerging startups. By conducting market research, identifying competitive threats, and developing strategies to differentiate their offerings, they can capture market share and stay ahead of competitors.

e) Financial Management: Companies like Berkshire Hathaway manage finances by maintaining financial discipline, monitoring cash flow, and seeking additional funding sources when needed. By creating financial projections, setting budgets, and conducting regular financial reviews, they can address challenges related to financial management and ensure long-term sustainability.

The above examples demonstrate how strategic planning, adaptability, and innovation are key factors in overcoming challenges and seizing opportunities for growth and expansion in dynamic business environments.

CHAPTER ELEVEN

ENTREPRENEURIAL LEADERSHIP

Entrepreneurial leadership is a style of leadership that is characterized by innovation, risk-taking, and a strong vision for the future. Entrepreneurs who exhibit this type of leadership are often driven by a desire to create something new, disrupt existing industries, and drive growth and change within their organizations.

Entrepreneurial Leadership Style

One of the key aspects of entrepreneurial leadership is the ability to think creatively and take calculated risks. Entrepreneurs are willing to step outside of their comfort zones, challenge the status quo, and pursue new opportunities that others may overlook. They are not afraid to fail and see setbacks as learning experiences that can ultimately lead to success.

Entrepreneurial leaders also possess a strong vision for the future and are able to inspire and motivate others to work towards a common goal. They are excellent communicators who can effectively articulate their vision and rally their team around it. They are also adept at building strong relationships with stakeholders, investors, and customers, which is crucial for the success of any entrepreneurial venture.

In addition, entrepreneurial leaders are adaptable and resilient in the face of challenges and uncertainty. They are able to pivot quickly in response to changing market conditions and are constantly seeking out new opportunities for growth and expansion. They are also committed to continuous learning and self-improvement, constantly seeking new knowledge and skills to stay ahead in a rapidly evolving business landscape.

Overall, entrepreneurial leadership is essential for driving innovation, growth, and success in today's dynamic and competitive business environment. Entrepreneurs who embody this style of leadership are able to navigate uncertainty, overcome obstacles, and create lasting impact through their ability to think creatively, take risks, and inspire others to follow their lead.

Characteristics of Successful Entrepreneurial Leaders

Successful entrepreneurial leaders possess a unique set of characteristics that set them apart and enable them to drive innovation, growth, and success in their ventures. These characteristics include the following:

1. Visionary: Successful entrepreneurial leaders have a clear and compelling vision for the future of their organizations. They are able to see opportunities where others see challenges and can articulate a path forward that inspires and motivates their team.

2. Risk-takers: Entrepreneurial leaders are not afraid to take calculated risks in pursuit of their goals. They understand that innovation and growth often require stepping outside of one's comfort zone and are willing to embrace uncertainty and failure as part of the entrepreneurial journey.

3. Resilient: Successful entrepreneurial leaders are resilient in the face of setbacks and challenges. They are able to bounce back from failures, learn from their mistakes, and adapt quickly to changing circumstances.

4. Creative and innovative: Entrepreneurial leaders are creative thinkers who are constantly seeking out new ideas and approaches to solving problems. They are not bound by conventional thinking and are willing to disrupt existing industries and business models.

5. Passionate: Successful entrepreneurial leaders are passionate about their work and deeply committed to their vision. Their passion is infectious and inspires others to share in their enthusiasm and dedication.

6. Decisive: Entrepreneurial leaders are decisive and able to make tough decisions quickly and confidently. They are not afraid to take action and are able to move forward with conviction even in the face of uncertainty.

7. Collaborative: Successful entrepreneurial leaders understand the value of collaboration and are able to build strong relationships with their team, partners, and stakeholders. They are effective communicators who are able to inspire and motivate others to work towards a common goal.

8. Adaptive: Entrepreneurial leaders are adaptable and able to pivot quickly in response to changing market conditions. They are constantly scanning the horizon for new opportunities and are willing to adjust their strategies and plans as needed.

9. Continuous learners: Successful entrepreneurial leaders are committed to lifelong learning and self-improvement. They seek out new knowledge and skills to stay ahead in a rapidly evolving business landscape and are open to feedback and constructive criticism.

10. Ethical and values-driven: Entrepreneurial leaders operate with integrity and are guided by a strong set of values. They prioritize ethical behavior and social responsibility in their decision-making and strive to create positive impact in their communities and industries.

In conclusion, the characteristics of successful entrepreneurial leaders are multifaceted and encompass a combination of vision, risk-taking, resilience, creativity, passion, decisiveness, collaboration, adaptability, continuous learning, and ethical values. By embodying these traits, entrepreneurial leaders can navigate the challenges of entrepreneurship and create lasting impact through their ventures.

Developing Leadership Skills for Driving Innovation and Growth

Developing leadership skills for driving innovation and growth is essential for entrepreneurial success in today's rapidly changing business landscape. Here are some key strategies for entrepreneurs to enhance their leadership skills in order to foster innovation and drive growth:

1. Embrace a Growth Mindset: Adopting a growth mindset is crucial for entrepreneurial leaders looking to drive innovation and growth. This mindset involves a belief that abilities and intelligence can be developed through dedication and hard work. By approaching challenges with a growth mindset, leaders can inspire creativity, resilience, and a willingness to take risks within their teams.

2. Foster a Culture of Innovation: As a leader, it is important to create an organizational culture that values and encourages innovation. This can be achieved by promoting creativity, experimentation, and learning from failure. Encourage your team members to think outside the box, share their ideas, and collaborate on innovative solutions to business challenges.

3. Develop Emotional Intelligence: Emotional intelligence is a key leadership skill that enables entrepreneurs to understand and manage their own emotions, as well as those of others. By developing emotional intelligence, leaders can build strong relationships with their team members, communicate effectively, and inspire trust and collaboration within the organization.

4. Encourage Continuous Learning: Successful entrepreneurial leaders are committed to lifelong learning and self-improvement. They seek out opportunities to expand their knowledge, skills, and perspectives through reading, attending workshops, networking with other industry professionals, and seeking feedback from mentors and advisors. By continuously learning and growing, leaders can stay ahead of industry trends and drive innovation within their organizations. Lifelong learning is not just a buzzword in the entrepreneurial world; it is a fundamental principle that fuels innovation, growth, and success.

5. Lead by Example: As a leader, it is important to model the behaviors and attitudes that you want to see in your team. Demonstrate a strong work ethic, a positive attitude, and a commitment to excellence in everything you do. By leading by example, you can inspire your team members to follow suit and strive for innovation and growth in their own work.

6. Empower and Delegate: Effective leaders empower their team members by delegating responsibilities and giving them the autonomy to make decisions and take ownership of their work. By empowering your team members, you can foster a sense of accountability, creativity, and innovation within the organization.

7. Build a Diverse and Inclusive Team: Diversity and inclusion are key drivers of innovation and growth within organizations. By building a team with diverse backgrounds, perspectives, and experiences, you can foster creativity, collaboration, and the generation of new ideas. Encourage open communication and respect for different viewpoints to create a culture of inclusivity and innovation.

8. Set Clear Goals and Expectations: As a leader, it is important to set clear goals and expectations for your team members to ensure alignment and focus. Clearly communicate the vision, mission, and objectives of the organization, and provide your team with the resources and support they need to achieve success. Regularly review progress towards goals and provide feedback to keep your team motivated and on track.

By developing these leadership skills and strategies, entrepreneurial leaders can create a culture of innovation, drive growth, and position their organizations for long-term success in today's competitive business environment.

Application of Entrepreneurial Leadership to Real-world Business Circumstances

The application of entrepreneurial leadership to real-world business circumstances is essential for driving innovation, growth, and success in today's competitive marketplace. Entrepreneurial leaders possess a unique set of skills and qualities that enable them to navigate challenges, seize opportunities, and create value for their organizations. Here are some ways in which entrepreneurial leadership can be applied to real-world business circumstances:

1. Vision and Strategic Planning: Entrepreneurial leaders are visionaries who have a clear sense of purpose and direction for their organizations. They are able to set ambitious goals, develop strategic plans, and chart a course for growth and success. By articulating a compelling vision and creating a roadmap for achieving it, entrepreneurial leaders can inspire their teams, attract investors, and differentiate their businesses in the marketplace.

2. Risk-Taking and Innovation: Entrepreneurial leaders are willing to take calculated risks and embrace innovation in order to stay ahead of the competition. They are not afraid to challenge the status quo, experiment with new ideas, and disrupt existing business models. By encouraging a culture of creativity and experimentation within their organizations, entrepreneurial leaders can drive innovation, foster a spirit of entrepreneurship, and create new opportunities for growth.

3. Resilience and Adaptability: Entrepreneurial leaders are live or cope with unpleasant situations in the face of adversity and able to adapt to changing market conditions. They understand that setbacks and failures are an inevitable part of the entrepreneurial journey and are able to bounce back quickly from challenges. By remaining active, flexible, and open to new possibilities, entrepreneurial leaders can review their strategies, adjust to unforeseen circumstances, and position their organizations for long-term success.

4. Customer-Centric Approach: Entrepreneurial leaders prioritize customer needs and preferences in their decision-making processes. They are committed to delivering value to their customers, building strong relationships, and exceeding expectations. By listening to customer feedback, understanding market trends, and anticipating future demands, entrepreneurial leaders can create products and services that resonate with their target audience and drive customer loyalty and satisfaction.

5. Team Building and Collaboration: Entrepreneurial leaders understand the importance of building a strong team and fostering a culture of collaboration within their organizations. They are able to attract top talent, inspire their employees, and empower them to achieve their full potential. By creating a supportive and inclusive work environment, entrepreneurial leaders can harness the collective expertise and creativity of their team members to drive innovation, solve complex problems, and achieve shared goals.

6. Ethical Leadership and Social Responsibility: Entrepreneurial leaders operate with integrity, transparency, and a strong sense of social responsibility. They prioritize ethical behavior, sustainability, and corporate citizenship in their decision-making processes. By demonstrating a commitment to ethical leadership and responsible business practices, entrepreneurial leaders can build trust with their stakeholders, enhance their reputation, and create positive impact in their communities.

In conclusion, the application of entrepreneurial leadership to real-world business circumstances is essential for driving innovation, growth, and success in today's dynamic and competitive business environment. By embodying the qualities of visionary leadership, risk-taking, resilience, customer-centricity, team building, and ethical responsibility, entrepreneurial leaders can create value, differentiate their organizations, and achieve sustainable growth and success.

CHAPTER TWELVE

ENTREPRENEURSHIP AND CORPORATE INNOVATION

The Relationship between Entrepreneurship and Corporate Innovation

The difference between entrepreneurship and corporate Innovation is very clear. Entrepreneurship is often associated with startups and new ventures, while corporate innovation refers to the process of developing and implementing new ideas, products, services, or business models within established organizations.

Entrepreneurship and corporate innovation are closely intertwined concepts that play a significant role in driving business growth, competitiveness, and sustainability. The relationship between entrepreneurship and corporate innovation can be characterized by the following key aspects:

1. Entrepreneurial Mindset: Both entrepreneurship and corporate innovation require an entrepreneurial mindset characterized by creativity, risk-taking, adaptability, and a willingness to challenge the status quo. Entrepreneurs and corporate innovators share a common drive to identify opportunities, solve problems, and drive change within their respective contexts.

2. Organizational Culture: Cultivating an entrepreneurial culture within a corporate environment is essential for fostering innovation and driving growth. Companies that encourage employees to think and act like entrepreneurs, experiment with new ideas and take calculated risks, are more likely to succeed in driving innovation and staying ahead of the competition.

3. Resource Allocation: Entrepreneurship and corporate innovation involve the allocation of resources, including financial, human, and technological assets, to support the development and implementation of new initiatives. Companies that prioritize innovation through dedicated budgets, cross-functional teams, and strategic partnerships are better positioned to drive sustainable growth and competitive advantage.

4. Collaboration and Partnerships: Collaboration and partnerships play a crucial role in fostering entrepreneurship and driving corporate innovation. By engaging with external stakeholders, such as startups, industry experts, academia, and customers, companies can access new ideas, technologies, and market insights that fuel innovation and drive business transformation.

5. Risk Management: Both entrepreneurship and corporate innovation involve taking risks, whether in launching a new product, entering a new market, or implementing a disruptive business model. Companies need to balance risk-taking with effective risk management strategies to mitigate potential challenges, optimize resource allocation, and maximize the chances of success in their innovation initiatives.

6. Market Dynamics: Understanding market dynamics, customer needs, and competitive landscapes is essential for successful entrepreneurship and corporate innovation. Companies that engage in market research, customer feedback, and trend analysis can identify emerging opportunities, anticipate industry shifts, and develop innovative solutions that resonate with target audiences.

7. Scalability and Sustainability: While entrepreneurship often focuses on launching and scaling new ventures, (while) corporate innovation aims to drive sustainable growth and long-term success

within established organizations. Companies that integrate entrepreneurship and innovation into their strategic planning processes can create a culture of continuous improvement, adaptability, and resilience to navigate evolving market dynamics and stay competitive.

The relationship between entrepreneurship and corporate innovation is symbiotic, with both concepts complementing each other to drive business success and create value for stakeholders. By embracing an entrepreneurial mindset, fostering a culture of innovation, allocating resources strategically, fostering collaboration, managing risks effectively, understanding market dynamics, and prioritizing scalability and sustainability, companies can leverage the synergies between entrepreneurship and corporate innovation to drive growth, competitiveness, and long-term success in today's dynamic business environment.

Strategies for Fostering a Culture of Innovation within Established Organizations

Fostering a culture of innovation within established organizations is essential for driving growth, staying competitive, and adapting to changing market dynamics. To cultivate an environment that encourages creativity, experimentation, and continuous improvement, organizations can implement the following strategies:

1. Leadership Support: Leadership plays a crucial role in shaping the organizational culture and setting the tone for innovation. Senior executives and managers should actively champion innovation, communicate its importance, and allocate resources to support innovative initiatives. By demonstrating a commitment to

innovation, leaders can inspire employees to embrace new ideas and take calculated risks.

2. Clear Vision and Objectives: Establishing a clear vision and objectives for innovation helps align efforts across the organization and provide a sense of purpose for employees. Organizations should define strategic goals, key performance indicators, and milestones for innovation initiatives to track progress, measure impact, and ensure alignment with business objectives.

3. Encouraging Risk-Taking: Creating a safe environment for risk-taking and experimentation is essential for fostering innovation. Organizations should encourage employees to challenge the status quo, explore new ideas, and learn from failures. By celebrating both successes and setbacks, organizations can create a culture that values learning, resilience, and continuous improvement.

4. Empowering Employees: Empowering employees to contribute ideas, share feedback, and take ownership of innovation initiatives is key to fostering a culture of innovation. Organizations should provide opportunities for cross-functional collaboration, skill development, and autonomy to enable employees to unleash their creativity, drive change, and make a meaningful impact within the organization.

5. Rewarding and Recognizing Innovation: Recognizing and rewarding employees for their innovative contributions reinforces a culture of innovation and motivates continued creativity. Organizations can implement reward systems, recognition programs, and incentives to acknowledge and celebrate innovative ideas, projects, and outcomes. By highlighting the value of

innovation, organizations can inspire a sense of pride, engagement, and commitment among employees.

6. Providing Resources and Support: Investing in resources, tools, and infrastructure that support innovation is essential for enabling employees to bring their ideas to life. Organizations should allocate budgets, provide access to technology, and offer training programs to enhance employees' innovation capabilities and facilitate the implementation of innovative solutions.

7. Promoting Collaboration and Diversity: Encouraging collaboration across teams, departments, and disciplines fosters a diverse range of perspectives, ideas, and approaches to problem-solving. Organizations should create opportunities for knowledge sharing, brainstorming sessions, and cross-functional projects to stimulate creativity, drive innovation, and *break down silos* within the organization. Breaking down silos is breaking down barriers or divisions between different departments or teams within an organization to encourage collaboration and communication.

8. Continuous Learning and Improvement: Embracing a culture of continuous learning and improvement is critical for sustaining innovation over time. Organizations should foster a growth mindset, encourage feedback and reflection, and promote a culture of experimentation and iteration. By embracing a culture of learning, organizations can adapt to changing market conditions, seize new opportunities, and drive ongoing innovation.

In conclusion, fostering a culture of innovation within established organizations requires a strategic and holistic approach that involves leadership support, clear vision and objectives, risk-taking, employee empowerment, rewards and recognition, resource allocation, collaboration, diversity, continuous learning, and improvement. By implementing these strategies, organizations can create an environment that nurtures creativity, drives growth, and positions them for long-term success in today's dynamic business landscape.

CHAPTER THIRTEEN

ENTREPRENEURSHIP AND SOCIAL IMPACT

We are now on Entrepreneurship and Social Impact. The first section of this chapter examines the role of entrepreneurship in driving social change. The second one is on opportunities for creating sustainable and socially responsible businesses.

The Role of Entrepreneurship in Driving Social Change

Entrepreneurship plays a crucial role in driving social change by creating innovative solutions to address pressing social issues. Entrepreneurs are often driven by a desire to make a positive impact on society and are willing to take risks to bring about change.

One way in which entrepreneurship drives social change is through the creation of social enterprises. These are businesses that have a social mission at their core and seek to address social or environmental issues while also generating profit. Social enterprises often operate in sectors that traditional businesses may overlook, such as providing affordable healthcare, education, or clean energy solutions to underserved communities.

Entrepreneurs also drive social change by challenging the status quo and disrupting outdated systems. By introducing new ideas, technologies, and business models, entrepreneurs can revolutionize industries and create more inclusive and sustainable solutions. For example, companies like TOMS Shoes and Warby Parker have pioneered the concept of "buy one, give one" to provide products to those in need while also running profitable businesses.

Moreover, entrepreneurship can empower marginalized communities and individuals by providing opportunities for economic independence and social mobility. By starting their own businesses, individuals can create jobs, build wealth, and contribute to the local economy. This can help reduce poverty, inequality, and social exclusion in communities around the world.

In conclusion, entrepreneurship is a powerful force for driving social change. By fostering innovation, creating social enterprises, challenging the status quo, and empowering individuals, entrepreneurs can make a significant impact on society and help build a more sustainable and equitable future for all.

Opportunities for Creating Sustainable and Socially Responsible Businesses

There are numerous opportunities for creating sustainable and socially responsible businesses in today's market. As consumers become more conscious of the environmental and social impact of their purchasing decisions, there is a growing demand for businesses that prioritize sustainability and social responsibility. Here are some key opportunities for entrepreneurs looking to create businesses that are both profitable and purpose-driven:

1. Sustainable products and services: There is a growing market for products and services that are environmentally friendly, ethically sourced, and produced using sustainable practices. Businesses that offer eco-friendly alternatives to traditional products, such as reusable water bottles, organic skincare products, or electric vehicles, can capitalize on this trend.

2. Green technology and renewable energy: The shift towards renewable energy sources and sustainable technologies presents a significant opportunity for entrepreneurs. Businesses that develop innovative solutions for clean energy, energy efficiency, waste management, and water conservation can make a positive impact on the environment while also generating revenue.

3. Social enterprises: Social enterprises combine the mission-driven approach of non-profit organizations with the revenue-generating model of for-profit businesses. By addressing social issues such as poverty, education, healthcare, or homelessness, social enterprises can create sustainable business models that have a lasting impact on society.

4. Circular economy and waste reduction: Businesses that focus on reducing waste, promoting recycling, and adopting a circular economy approach can create value from products and materials that would otherwise be discarded. By designing products for longevity, reusability, and recyclability, entrepreneurs can minimize their environmental footprint and contribute to a more sustainable future.

5. Ethical supply chains and fair trade: Consumers are increasingly concerned about the ethical sourcing of products and the treatment of workers in the supply chain. Businesses that prioritize fair trade practices, transparency, and accountability in their supply chains can differentiate themselves in the market and build trust with socially conscious consumers.

Overall, there are ample opportunities for entrepreneurs to create sustainable and socially responsible businesses that align with the values of today's consumers. By focusing on environmental stewardship, social impact, and ethical business practices, entrepreneurs can not only drive positive change in the world but also build successful and resilient businesses for the future.

CHAPTER FOURTEEN

ENTREPRENEURSHIP AND GLOBALIZATION

Entrepreneurship in a globalized economy presents both challenges and opportunities for aspiring business owners. Globalization has transformed the way businesses operate, connect, and compete in the international marketplace.

Challenges and Opportunities of Entrepreneurship in a Globalized Economy

Here are some key challenges and opportunities that entrepreneurs may encounter in a globalized economy:

Challenges:

1. Increased competition: Globalization has opened up markets to businesses from around the world, leading to heightened competition. Entrepreneurs must navigate a crowded marketplace and differentiate their products or services to stand out among competitors.

2. Cultural differences: Doing business in a globalized economy requires an understanding of diverse cultures, customs, and business practices. Entrepreneurs may face challenges in building relationships, negotiating deals, and communicating effectively across cultural boundaries.

3. Regulatory complexities: Operating in multiple countries means dealing with a variety of regulatory frameworks, tax laws, and compliance requirements. Entrepreneurs must stay informed

about legal and regulatory changes in different markets to ensure compliance and avoid potential risks.

4. Supply chain disruptions: Global supply chains are vulnerable to disruptions such as natural disasters, political instability, or economic crises. Entrepreneurs must have contingency plans in place to mitigate the impact of supply chain disruptions and ensure business continuity.

Opportunities:

1. Access to new markets: Globalization provides entrepreneurs with access to a larger customer base and new market opportunities. By expanding their reach beyond domestic borders, entrepreneurs can tap into new sources of revenue and growth potential.

2. Collaboration and partnerships: Globalization enables entrepreneurs to collaborate with international partners, suppliers, and distributors to leverage expertise, resources, and market reach. Strategic partnerships can help entrepreneurs scale their businesses more efficiently and enter new markets.

3. Innovation and technology: Advances in technology and communication have made it easier for entrepreneurs to develop innovative products, (and) reach global audiences, and operate remotely. Entrepreneurs can leverage technology to streamline operations, improve customer engagement, and drive business growth.

4. Talent acquisition: Globalization allows entrepreneurs to access a diverse talent pool from around the world. By hiring (They can hire) skilled professionals from different backgrounds and

cultures, entrepreneurs can foster creativity, innovation, and global perspective within their organizations.

In conclusion, entrepreneurship in a globalized economy presents both challenges and opportunities for business owners. By understanding the complexities of operating in a global marketplace and leveraging the opportunities that globalization offers, entrepreneurs can build successful and sustainable businesses that thrive in an interconnected world.

Strategies for Expanding into International Markets

Expanding into international markets can be a lucrative opportunity for entrepreneurs looking to grow their business and reach a global audience. However, entering new markets comes with its own set of challenges and complexities. Here are some key strategies for entrepreneurs to consider when expanding into international markets:

1. Market research and analysis: Before entering a new market, it is essential to conduct thorough market research to understand the local business environment, consumer preferences, competition, regulatory requirements, and *cultural nuances*. Cultural nuances are subtle or specific aspects of a culture that may affect communication, behavior, or decision-making. This will help entrepreneurs identify opportunities, assess risks, and develop a targeted market entry strategy.

2. Establish partnerships and alliances: Collaborating with local partners, distributors, or agents can help entrepreneurs navigate the complexities of international markets, build relationships with key stakeholders, and leverage local expertise. Partnerships can

also provide access to distribution networks, market insights, and resources that are essential for successful market entry.

3. Adapt products and services: Entrepreneurs should tailor their products or services to meet the specific needs and preferences of the target market. This may involve customizing features, packaging, pricing, or marketing strategies to align with local tastes, regulations, and cultural norms. Adapting to local market conditions can enhance product relevance and competitiveness in international markets.

4. Develop a strong brand presence: Building brand awareness and credibility in international markets is crucial for attracting customers and establishing a competitive position. Entrepreneurs should invest in localized marketing and branding efforts, such as multilingual websites, social media campaigns, and culturally relevant messaging, to engage with target audiences and differentiate their brand in the global marketplace.

5. Manage logistics and supply chain: Efficient logistics and supply chain management are essential for delivering products or services to international customers in a timely and cost-effective manner. Entrepreneurs should optimize their supply chain, distribution channels, and inventory management processes to ensure smooth operations across borders and minimize logistical challenges.

6. Compliance and regulatory considerations: Entrepreneurs expanding into international markets must comply with local laws, regulations, and trade policies. It is important to understand the legal requirements, tax implications, import/export restrictions, and intellectual property protections in the target market to avoid compliance issues and legal risks.

7. Invest in cultural intelligence and talent development: *Cultural intelligence* and intercultural competence are critical for successfully navigating international markets. Cultural intelligence refers to the ability to understand and navigate different cultural contexts effectively.

Entrepreneurs should invest in cross-cultural training for their team members, develop cultural awareness and sensitivity, and build diverse and inclusive organizational cultures that reflect the global nature of their business.

In conclusion, expanding into international markets requires careful planning, strategic decision-making, and a deep understanding of the local business landscape. By following these strategies and adapting to the unique challenges and opportunities of international expansion, entrepreneurs can successfully grow their business and establish a strong presence in global markets.

CHAPTER FIFTEEN

ENTREPRENEURIAL FINANCE

This chapter has three sections. The first one covers funding options for entrepreneurs. You know, you cannot do a business without some form of funding, no matter small. The second one is on financial planning and management, while the third one focuses on valuation and exit strategies.

Funding Options for Entrepreneurs

This section explores the various sources of funding available to entrepreneurs, including bootstrapping, angel investors, venture capital, crowdfunding, bank loans, and government grants. It also mentions the advantages and disadvantages of each funding option.

Securing adequate funding is a critical step for entrepreneurs looking to launch or grow their business ventures. Understanding the various funding options available and selecting the most suitable sources of capital is essential for ensuring financial sustainability and driving business success. Here are some common funding options for entrepreneurs:

1. Bootstrapping:
Bootstrapping, also known as self-funding, involves using personal savings, credit cards, or assets to finance the business. This funding option gives entrepreneurs full control over their business and minimizes the need to rely on external investors. While bootstrapping can be a cost-effective way to start a business, it may limit the growth potential and scalability of the venture due to resource constraints.

2. Angel Investors:
Angel investors are affluent individuals who provide capital to early-stage startups in exchange for equity ownership. These investors typically offer not only financial support but also valuable expertise, industry connections, and mentorship to the entrepreneur. Securing funding from angel investors can be beneficial for startups seeking strategic guidance and networking opportunities to accelerate growth. However, entrepreneurs should be prepared to give up a portion of ownership and decision-making control in exchange for angel investment.

3. Venture Capital:
Venture capital (VC) firms invest in high-growth startups with the potential for significant returns. VC funding is typically provided in exchange for equity ownership and involves a rigorous due diligence process to assess the business's growth prospects, market potential, and management team. Venture capital can provide startups with substantial capital to scale their operations, enter new markets, and achieve rapid growth. However, securing VC funding can be competitive, and entrepreneurs may need to demonstrate a strong business model and *growth trajectory* to attract VC investment. Growth trajectory refers to the path and rate at which a business expands over time.

4. Crowdfunding:
Crowdfunding platforms allow entrepreneurs to raise capital from a large number of individual investors or backers through online campaigns. Crowdfunding offers a way to validate business ideas, build a community of supporters, and access funding without giving up equity. There are different types of crowdfunding, including rewards-based crowdfunding, equity crowdfunding, and donation-based crowdfunding, each with its unique benefits and

considerations. Entrepreneurs should carefully plan and execute crowdfunding campaigns to engage backers and achieve funding goals successfully.

5. Bank Loans:
Traditional bank loans are a common funding option for entrepreneurs looking to finance their business through debt. Banks offer various types of loans, such as term loans, lines of credit, and Small Business Administration (SBA) loans, to support business operations, expansion, or capital investments. However, bank loans usually require collateral, a solid credit history, and a well-developed business plan to secure financing. While bank loans provide entrepreneurs with access to capital at competitive interest rates, they also involve repayment obligations and financial risk.

In conclusion, entrepreneurs should carefully evaluate their funding needs, business objectives, and risk tolerance to select the most suitable funding options for their ventures. Don't let the fear of financial risks hold you back from chasing your entrepreneurial dreams. Embrace the challenges, learn from failures, and watch your financial success soar. By exploring a combination of funding sources and aligning their funding strategy with their long-term business goals, entrepreneurs can secure the necessary capital to fuel growth, innovation, and success.

Financial Planning and Management

This section focuses on the importance of financial planning and management for entrepreneurs to achieve their business goals and objectives. It covers issues such as budgeting, cash flow management, financial forecasting, financial reporting and analysis, and risk assessment.

Effective financial planning and management are essential for the long-term success and sustainability of a business. By establishing sound financial strategies, monitoring key performance indicators, and making informed financial decisions, entrepreneurs can optimize their financial resources, mitigate risks, and drive business growth. Here, we discuss key considerations for financial planning and management in the context of entrepreneurial ventures:

1. Budgeting and Forecasting:
Budgeting and forecasting are fundamental components of financial planning that help entrepreneurs set financial goals, allocate resources effectively, and anticipate future cash flow needs. By creating a detailed budget that outlines revenue projections, expenses, and capital requirements, entrepreneurs can track financial performance, identify potential cost savings opportunities, and make informed decisions to achieve financial objectives. Regularly updating financial forecasts based on market trends, business performance, and external factors enables entrepreneurs to adapt their strategies and allocate resources strategically to support business growth.

2. Cash Flow Management:
Cash flow management is crucial for ensuring the financial health and liquidity of a business. Entrepreneurs should monitor cash inflows and outflows, optimize working capital, and manage payment cycles to maintain a positive cash flow position. By implementing cash flow forecasting, tracking *receivables* and *payables*, and identifying cash flow bottlenecks, entrepreneurs can proactively address cash flow challenges and prevent cash shortages that may impact business operations. Receivables are amounts owed to a company by customers for goods or services

provided on credit, while payables are Amounts owed by a company to suppliers or vendors for goods or services received on credit.

Effective cash flow management enables entrepreneurs to meet financial obligations, invest in growth opportunities, and weather financial uncertainties with confidence.

3. Financial Reporting and Analysis:
Financial reporting and analysis provide entrepreneurs with valuable insights into the financial performance and health of their business. By generating accurate and timely financial statements, such as *income statements*, *balance sheets*, and *cash flow statements*, entrepreneurs can assess profitability, liquidity, and solvency metrics to inform decision-making. An income statement is a financial statement that shows a company's revenues, expenses, and profits over a specific period. A balance sheet is a financial statement that provides a snapshot of a company's assets, liabilities, and shareholders' equity at a specific point in time, while a cash flow statement is financial statement that shows the inflow and outflow of cash in a business over a specific period.

Conducting financial analysis, *ratio analysis*, and *variance analysis* helps entrepreneurs identify trends, evaluate performance against benchmarks, and pinpoint areas for improvement. Ratio analysis refers to the process of analyzing and interpreting financial ratios to evaluate a company's performance and financial health, while variance analysis is a technique used to compare actual financial performance against planned or budgeted performance to identify differences and analyze their causes. By leveraging financial data and analytics, entrepreneurs can make data-driven decisions, optimize resource allocation, and drive financial efficiency and profitability.

4. Risk Management:
Risk management is an integral part of financial planning and management that involves identifying, assessing, and mitigating financial risks that may impact business operations and objectives. Entrepreneurs should conduct risk assessments, establish risk mitigation strategies, and implement internal controls to safeguard assets, protect against financial losses, and ensure compliance with regulatory requirements. By proactively managing risks related to market volatility, credit risk, operational risk, and cybersecurity threats, entrepreneurs can enhance financial resilience, build stakeholder trust, and sustain long-term business success.

Effective financial planning and management are essential for entrepreneurs to optimize financial performance, mitigate risks, and achieve sustainable growth. By adopting best practices in budgeting, cash flow management, financial reporting, and risk management, entrepreneurs can enhance financial transparency, accountability, and strategic decision-making to drive business success in a dynamic and competitive business environment.

Valuation and Exit Strategies

Valuation and exit strategies play a critical role in the strategic planning and long-term success of entrepreneurial ventures. Valuation involves determining the worth of a business based on various factors, such as financial performance, market conditions, growth potential, and *industry comparables*. Industry comparables are companies within the same industry that are used for comparison in financial analysis. Exit strategies focus on planning how entrepreneurs will exit or transition out of their businesses, whether through a sale, merger, IPO, or other strategic options.

Here, we discuss key considerations for valuation and exit strategies in the context of entrepreneurial ventures:

1. Valuation Methods:
Entrepreneurs can use various valuation methods to determine the value of their business, such as the *discounted cash flow (DCF) method, comparable company analysis, precedent transactions analysis,* and *asset-based valuation.* Discounted Cash Flow (DCF) Method is a valuation method used to estimate the value of an investment based on its projected future cash flows, discounted to present value. Comparable Company Analysis is a valuation method that compares a company's financial metrics to those of similar publicly traded companies. Precedent Transactions Analysis is a valuation method that uses the prices paid in past M&A transactions involving similar companies to estimate the value of a target company. Asset-Based Valuation is a valuation method that determines a company's value based on its tangible and intangible assets.

Each valuation method has its strengths and limitations, and the choice of method may depend on the nature of the business, industry dynamics, growth prospects, and exit timeline. By conducting a comprehensive valuation analysis, entrepreneurs can assess the fair market value of their business, attract potential investors or buyers, and negotiate favorable terms for financing or exit transactions.

2. Exit Planning:
Exit planning involves developing a strategic roadmap for transitioning out of the business and realizing value for stakeholders, such as founders, investors, and employees. Entrepreneurs should consider their long-term goals, financial

objectives, and timeline for exiting the business when crafting an exit strategy. Common exit strategies include selling the business to a strategic buyer, merging with a competitor, pursuing an *initial public offering* (IPO), or passing the business to a family member or successor. IPO is the process by which a private company offers its shares to the public for the first time. By proactively planning for an exit, entrepreneurs can maximize value, minimize risks, and ensure a smooth transition that aligns with their personal and professional aspirations.

3. Value Drivers:
Identifying and enhancing *value drivers* are essential for maximizing the valuation of a business and attracting potential investors or acquirers. Value drivers are factors that significantly impact the value of a business or investment. They may include strong revenue growth, recurring revenue streams, proprietary technology or intellectual property, a loyal customer base, experienced management team, scalable business model, and competitive advantage in the market. By focusing on strengthening value drivers, optimizing operational efficiency, and differentiating the business in the marketplace, entrepreneurs can increase the attractiveness of their business to potential buyers and investors, ultimately driving a higher valuation and favorable exit outcomes.

4. Due Diligence:
Conducting thorough *due diligence* is critical during the valuation and exit process to assess the financial, operational, legal, and strategic aspects of the business. Due diligence refers to the process of investigating and evaluating a company or investment before making a decision. Buyers or investors may perform due diligence to evaluate the business's performance, risks, compliance, and growth potential before finalizing a transaction. Entrepreneurs

should prepare comprehensive due diligence documentation, address potential *red flags* or issues proactively, and collaborate with advisors, legal counsel, and financial experts to navigate the due diligence process effectively. Red flags are warning signs or indicators of potential problems or risks in a business or investment. By demonstrating transparency, integrity, and readiness for due diligence, entrepreneurs can build trust with potential buyers or investors and facilitate successful valuation and exit transactions.

In conclusion, valuation and exit strategies are essential components of strategic planning for entrepreneurial ventures, enabling entrepreneurs to assess the value of their business, plan for a successful exit, and maximize returns for stakeholders. By leveraging valuation methods, exit planning strategies, value drivers, and due diligence best practices, entrepreneurs can position their businesses for a successful exit and achieve their financial and strategic objectives in a competitive and dynamic business environment.

CHAPTER SIXTEEN

ARTIFICIAL INTELLIGENCE, BUSINESS, AND SOCIETY

Understanding the implications of AI on business and society is essential for entrepreneurs, business leaders, policymakers, and individuals. This chapter has four sections. The first one examines AI Applications in Business. The second one is on ethical and social implications of AI. You know, you should *embrace the power of AI in business, but never forget the human touch. Let technology enhance, not replace, the essence of human connection and empathy.*
The third section covers strategies for promoting ethical AI practices in business organizations. The last section deals with future trends and opportunities, it looks ahead to the future of AI in business and society, exploring emerging trends, opportunities, and challenges that are likely to shape the landscape in the coming years.

The intersection of Artificial Intelligence (AI), business, and society is a compelling and rapidly evolving field that is reshaping the way organizations operate, interact with customers, and impact communities. AI technologies have the potential to revolutionize industries, streamline processes, and drive innovation, but they also raise important ethical, social, and economic considerations that must be carefully navigated. Understanding the implications of AI on business and society is essential for entrepreneurs, business leaders, policymakers, and individuals alike as they navigate the opportunities and challenges presented by this transformative technology.

AI Applications in Business

This section explores the various ways in which AI is being applied in business contexts to enhance operations, improve decision-making, and drive competitive advantage. It delves into specific use cases of AI in areas such as marketing, finance, supply chain management, customer service, and product development, highlighting the benefits and challenges associated with implementing AI technologies in business settings.

AI has emerged as a transformative technology that offers a wide range of applications and opportunities for businesses to enhance efficiency, productivity, and decision-making. From automation and predictive analytics to personalized customer experiences and process optimization, AI has the potential to revolutionize various aspects of business operations. Here, we explore key considerations for leveraging AI applications in business to drive innovation, competitiveness, and growth:

1. Automation and Efficiency:
AI-driven automation technologies, such as *robotic process automation* (RPA), *chatbots, and virtual assistants,* enable businesses to streamline repetitive tasks, reduce manual errors, and improve operational efficiency. Robotic process automation is the use of software robots or bots to automate repetitive tasks and processes. A chatbot is a computer program designed to simulate conversation with human users, typically used for customer service or information retrieval, while a virtual assistant is an AI-powered software program that can assist users with tasks such as scheduling, reminders, and information retrieval.

By deploying AI-powered automation solutions, businesses can enhance productivity, accelerate workflows, and free up employees to focus on higher-value tasks that require creativity, critical thinking, and problem-solving. Automation also enables businesses to scale operations, handle increasing workloads, and adapt to changing market demands more effectively, ultimately driving cost savings and operational excellence.

2. Predictive Analytics and Insights:
AI-powered predictive analytics tools leverage machine learning algorithms to analyze vast amounts of data, identify patterns, trends, and correlations, and predict future outcomes or trends with a high degree of accuracy. Businesses can use predictive analytics to forecast sales, optimize inventory levels, anticipate customer behavior, and make data-driven decisions that drive business growth. By harnessing the power of AI for predictive analytics, businesses can gain valuable insights, mitigate risks, seize opportunities, and stay ahead of the competition in a rapidly evolving marketplace.

3. Personalized Customer Experiences:
AI technologies, such as *natural language processing* (NLP), *sentiment analysis*, and recommendation engines, enable businesses to deliver personalized and tailored customer experiences across various touchpoints, such as websites, mobile apps, and customer service interactions. NLP is a branch of AI that enables computers to understand, interpret, and generate human language. Sentiment analysis means the process of analyzing text to determine the sentiment or emotion expressed, often used in social media monitoring and customer feedback analysis. By leveraging AI for customer segmentation, behavioral analysis, and personalized recommendations, businesses can enhance customer engagement,

loyalty, and satisfaction. Personalization also enables businesses to anticipate customer needs, deliver targeted marketing campaigns, and build long-lasting relationships that drive customer retention and loyalty.

4. Process Optimization and Decision-Making:
AI applications, such as machine learning algorithms, optimization models, and prescriptive analytics, empower businesses to optimize complex processes, improve decision-making, and drive strategic outcomes. Businesses can use AI to optimize supply chain operations, pricing strategies, resource allocation, and risk management processes. By leveraging AI for data-driven insights, scenario analysis, and decision support, businesses can make informed decisions, optimize performance, and capitalize on opportunities to drive growth and profitability.

Conclusion

AI applications offer businesses a myriad of opportunities to drive innovation, competitiveness, and growth by leveraging automation, predictive analytics, personalized customer experiences, and process optimization. By embracing AI technologies and integrating them into business operations, entrepreneurs can unlock new possibilities, enhance operational efficiency, and stay ahead of the curve in a rapidly evolving business landscape. Using AI applications strategically can help businesses achieve sustainable growth, enhance customer satisfaction, and drive long-term success in a digital-first world where digital technologies and online channels play a central role in business operations and consumer interactions. Finally, AI is not just a tool for profit; it's a force for positive change in society. Harness its potential to drive innovation, inclusivity, and sustainable growth.

Ethical and Social Implications of AI

This section addresses the ethical considerations and societal impacts of AI adoption in business and beyond. It examines issues such as bias in AI algorithms, data privacy concerns, job displacement due to automation, and the broader societal implications of AI-driven decision-making. Additionally, it explores strategies for promoting ethical AI practices, ensuring transparency and accountability, and fostering responsible AI innovation that benefits society as a whole.

As artificial intelligence (AI) technologies continue to advance and permeate various aspects of society, there are growing concerns about the ethical and social implications of AI applications. It is crucial for businesses and organizations to consider the ethical implications of AI to ensure that these technologies are developed and deployed responsibly, ethically, and in a manner that upholds human values and rights. Here, we explore key considerations for addressing the ethical and social implications of AI to promote transparency, accountability, and fairness in AI-driven decision-making:

1. Bias and Discrimination:
One of the primary ethical concerns surrounding AI is the potential for bias and discrimination in AI algorithms and decision-making processes. AI systems can inadvertently perpetuate biases present in training data, leading to discriminatory outcomes in areas such as hiring, lending, and criminal justice. Businesses must proactively address bias in *AI algorithms* by ensuring diverse and representative training data, implementing bias detection and mitigation techniques, and promoting transparency in AI decision-making processes. AI Algorithms are Mathematical algorithms

used in artificial intelligence systems to process data and make decisions. By mitigating bias in AI systems, businesses can uphold fairness, equity, and inclusivity in their operations and mitigate potential harm to marginalized groups.

2. Privacy and Data Protection:
AI technologies often rely on vast amounts of data to train algorithms and make informed decisions, raising concerns about privacy, data protection, and consent. Businesses must prioritize data privacy and protection by implementing robust data governance practices, obtaining informed consent from users, and ensuring compliance with data protection regulations, such as the General Data Protection Regulation (GDPR). By safeguarding user data and respecting privacy rights, businesses can build trust with customers, enhance data security, and mitigate risks associated with data breaches and unauthorized data usage.

3. Accountability and Transparency:
AI systems can operate in complex and opaque ways, making it challenging to understand how decisions are made and who is responsible for the outcomes. Businesses must prioritize accountability and transparency in AI decision-making by implementing explainable AI techniques, documenting AI processes, and establishing clear lines of responsibility for AI-driven decisions. By promoting transparency and accountability in AI systems, businesses can enhance trust, enable human oversight, and ensure that AI technologies align with ethical principles and legal requirements.

4. Job Displacement and Socioeconomic Impact:
The widespread adoption of AI technologies has raised concerns about *job displacement*, automation of tasks, and the socioeconomic impact on workers and communities. Job Displacement refers to

the loss of jobs due to automation, technology, or other factors. Businesses must consider the potential impact of AI on employment, reskilling opportunities, and income inequality, and take proactive measures to mitigate negative consequences. By investing in workforce training, supporting job transitions, and fostering collaboration between humans and AI systems, businesses can harness AI technologies to enhance productivity, create new job opportunities, and drive economic growth while mitigating the impact on workers and communities.

In conclusion, addressing the ethical and social implications of AI is essential for businesses to build trust, ensure fairness, and promote responsible AI development and deployment. By prioritizing ethical considerations, such as bias mitigation, data privacy, accountability, and socioeconomic impact, businesses can harness the transformative power of AI technologies while upholding human values, rights, and dignity. By adopting ethical AI practices and engaging with stakeholders, businesses can navigate the complex ethical landscape of AI and contribute to a more inclusive, equitable, and sustainable future for society.

Strategies for Promoting Ethical AI Practices in Business Organizations

Promoting ethical AI practices in business organizations is crucial to ensure that AI technologies are developed and deployed responsibly. Here are some strategies that can help promote ethical AI practices within organizations:

1. Establish Clear Ethical Guidelines: Develop and communicate clear ethical guidelines and principles for the design, development, and deployment of AI technologies within the organization. These

guidelines should align with ethical standards, legal requirements, and the organization's values.

2. Ethics Training for AI Teams: Provide training and awareness programs on ethical considerations in AI development and implementation for employees working on AI projects. This training should cover topics such as bias, fairness, transparency, accountability, and data privacy.

3. Diverse and Inclusive Teams: Foster diversity and inclusion within AI teams to bring different perspectives and experiences to the development process. This can help identify and address biases and ensure that AI systems are designed to serve diverse user groups.

4. Ethical Impact Assessments: Conduct ethical impact assessments to evaluate the potential ethical implications of AI projects before deployment. This process should involve identifying and mitigating risks related to bias, discrimination, privacy violations, and other ethical concerns.

5. Transparency and Explainability: Ensure that AI algorithms and decision-making processes are transparent and explainable to users and stakeholders. Provide clear explanations of how AI systems work, how decisions are made, and how data is used to build trust and accountability.

6. Data Privacy and Security: Prioritize data privacy and security in AI projects by implementing robust data protection measures, obtaining user consent for data collection and processing, and complying with relevant data privacy regulations.

7. Fairness and Bias Mitigation: Implement measures to mitigate biases in AI algorithms and ensure fairness in decision-making processes. Regularly monitor and audit AI systems for bias and discrimination, and take corrective actions when necessary.

8. Human Oversight and Accountability: Maintain human oversight of AI systems to ensure that decisions are aligned with ethical guidelines and organizational values. Establish mechanisms for accountability and recourse in case of errors or ethical violations.

9. Collaboration and Sharing Best Practices: Collaborate with industry peers, experts, and stakeholders to share best practices, research findings, and lessons learned in promoting ethical AI practices. Engage in industry initiatives and standards development to drive ethical AI adoption.

10. Continuous Monitoring and Evaluation: Continuously monitor and evaluate the ethical implications of AI technologies in real-world applications. Collect feedback from users, stakeholders, and impacted communities to identify areas for improvement and address ethical concerns proactively.

By implementing these strategies, business organizations can promote ethical AI practices, build trust with stakeholders, and contribute to the responsible and sustainable development of AI technologies.

Future Trends and Opportunities

This section looks ahead to the future of AI in business and society, exploring emerging trends, opportunities, and challenges that are likely to shape the landscape in the coming years. It discusses topics such as the rise of AI-powered business models, the potential for AI to drive sustainability and social impact, the role of AI in shaping future work environments, and the importance of collaboration between businesses, governments, and civil society to harness the full potential of AI for the benefit of all stakeholders.

As businesses navigate an ever-evolving digital landscape, it is essential to anticipate future trends and opportunities to stay ahead of the curve, drive innovation, and capitalize on emerging possibilities. By identifying key trends and opportunities shaping the business landscape, entrepreneurs can position their organizations for success, adapt to changing market dynamics, and unlock new growth avenues. Here, we explore future trends and opportunities that businesses can leverage to drive sustainable growth, foster innovation, and create competitive advantages:

1. Digital Transformation:
The ongoing digital transformation is reshaping industries and business models, driving the adoption of digital technologies, *cloud computing,* and data analytics. Cloud Computing is the delivery of computing services over the internet, allowing users to access and store data and applications remotely. Businesses that embrace digital transformation can enhance operational efficiency, improve customer experiences, and unlock new revenue streams. By investing in digital capabilities, such as e-commerce platforms, data-driven insights, and automation tools, businesses can streamline operations, optimize processes, and adapt to changing market demands. Embracing digital transformation enables businesses to stay competitive, drive innovation, and meet evolving customer expectations in a *digital-first economy.* Digital-first economy is an economy where digital technologies and online

channels play a central role in business operations and consumer interactions.

2. Artificial Intelligence and Automation:
Artificial intelligence (AI) and automation technologies are revolutionizing industries, enabling businesses to automate repetitive tasks, enhance decision-making, and drive efficiency. Businesses can leverage AI and automation to optimize processes, personalize customer experiences, and unlock new insights from data. By integrating AI-driven solutions, such as chatbots, predictive analytics, and robotic process automation, businesses can streamline operations, reduce costs, and accelerate innovation. Embracing AI and automation presents opportunities for businesses to enhance productivity, drive growth, and gain a competitive edge in a rapidly changing marketplace.

3. Sustainability and ESG Initiatives:
The growing focus on sustainability, environmental, social, and governance (ESG) factors is reshaping business practices and consumer preferences. Businesses that prioritize sustainability initiatives, such as reducing carbon emissions, promoting diversity and inclusion, and supporting community engagement, can enhance brand reputation, attract socially conscious customers, and drive long-term value creation. By integrating sustainability practices into business operations, supply chains, and product development, businesses can mitigate risks, foster stakeholder trust, and capitalize on emerging opportunities in the green economy. Embracing sustainability and *ESG initiatives* enables businesses to create positive social impact, drive innovation, and differentiate themselves in a competitive marketplace. ESG initiatives are Environmental, Social, and Governance initiatives that focus on sustainable and responsible business practices

4. Remote Work and Digital Collaboration:
The shift towards remote work and digital collaboration has accelerated in recent years, driven by technological advancements, changing work preferences, and global events. Businesses that embrace remote work practices, *virtual collaboration tools,* and flexible work arrangements can enhance employee productivity, attract top talent, and reduce operational costs. Virtual collaboration tools are software and platforms that enable remote teams to collaborate and communicate effectively. By leveraging digital communication platforms, project management tools, and virtual collaboration technologies, businesses can empower remote teams, foster creativity, and adapt to the changing nature of work. Embracing remote work and digital collaboration presents opportunities for businesses to access a global talent pool, improve work-life balance, and drive organizational agility in a digital-first world.

In conclusion, by proactively identifying and capitalizing on future trends and opportunities, businesses can position themselves for success, drive innovation, and create sustainable growth in a dynamic and competitive business environment. By embracing digital transformation, AI and automation, sustainability initiatives, and remote work practices, businesses can adapt to changing market dynamics, meet evolving customer needs, and unlock new possibilities for growth and differentiation. By staying agile, innovative, and forward-thinking, businesses can navigate future trends and opportunities to thrive in a rapidly changing business landscape.

CHAPTER SEVENTEEN

BUSINESS PLAN AND APPLIED BUSINESS RESEARCH

There are four sections for this topic. Perhaps, you'll agree with me that The MBA digest book on Entrepreneurship and Innovation will be incomplete without this essential topic.

The first section for this topic explains key components of a business Plan. This section is important because *a well-researched business plan is the blueprint for success in entrepreneurship. Let data be your guide, creativity be your fuel, and determination be your engine.*

The second section deals with market analysis and strategy that includes market research findings, such as consumer trends, market size, growth opportunities, and competitive analysis.

Another section covers the significance of applied business research to entrepreneurs. We need this section because *in the world of business, research is the foundation on which successful ventures are built. You should, therefore, dive deep, analyze thoroughly, and watch your ideas transform into reality.*

The forth section treats data collection and analysis while the last one covers strategic recommendations.

Key Components of a Business Plan

A well-crafted business plan is a foundational document that serves as a roadmap for entrepreneurs to define their business goals, strategies, and operational plans. It plays a crucial role in guiding decision-making, securing funding, and measuring the success of a business venture. Applied business research, on the other hand, involves the systematic investigation of business-related issues, trends, and opportunities to inform strategic decision-making and enhance business performance. Integrating business plan development with applied business research can help entrepreneurs create informed, data-driven strategies that are tailored to their specific market environment and business objectives.

Businesses play a crucial role in driving economic growth, creating employment opportunities, fostering innovation, and meeting the needs of customers and society. By establishing a clear vision, setting strategic goals, and implementing effective business plans, entrepreneurs can build successful enterprises that contribute to the overall prosperity and well-being of communities. Here, we outline the key components of a business plan, highlighting the importance of each element in guiding business operations, attracting investors, and achieving long-term success:

1. Executive Summary:

The executive summary provides a concise overview of the business plan, outlining the company's mission, vision, key objectives, target market, competitive advantage, and financial projections. It serves as a snapshot of the business, capturing the essence of the venture and setting the stage for the rest of the plan. The executive summary is crucial for capturing the attention of potential investors, partners, and stakeholders, highlighting the business's value proposition and growth potential.

2. Business Description:

The business description provides a detailed overview of the company, its history, industry sector, products or services offered, target market, competitive landscape, and unique selling proposition. It articulates the business's value proposition, market positioning, and competitive advantage, setting the foundation for the business's strategic direction and growth trajectory. The business description helps stakeholders understand the nature of the business, its market opportunities, and its competitive strengths in the marketplace.

3. Market Analysis:

The market analysis section examines the industry landscape, market trends, customer needs, competitive forces, and target market segments. It involves conducting market research, analyzing market data, and identifying growth opportunities and market gaps. The market analysis helps businesses understand their target customers, assess market demand, evaluate competitors, and identify key success factors for market entry and growth. By conducting a comprehensive market analysis, businesses can develop effective marketing strategies, tailor their products or services to meet customer needs, and capitalize on market opportunities.

4. Marketing and Sales Strategy:

The marketing and sales strategy outlines how the business will promote its products or services, attract customers, and generate revenue. It includes marketing tactics, sales channels, pricing strategies, branding initiatives, and customer acquisition plans. The marketing and sales strategy helps businesses reach their target audience, build brand awareness, drive customer engagement, and achieve sales targets. By developing a robust marketing and sales strategy, businesses can effectively position their offerings in the market, differentiate themselves from competitors, and drive customer acquisition and retention.

5. Operations and Management:

The operations and management section details the organizational structure, key personnel, operational processes, production capabilities, and resource requirements of the business. It outlines how the business will be managed, the roles and responsibilities of team members, and the operational workflows and systems in place. The operations and management section helps businesses establish efficient processes, optimize resource allocation, and ensure smooth day-to-day operations. By defining clear roles and responsibilities, establishing effective communication channels, and implementing robust operational procedures, businesses can enhance productivity, minimize risks, and achieve operational excellence.

6. Financial Projections:

The financial projections section presents the financial forecasts, budget estimates, revenue projections, and cash flow analysis of the business. It includes income statements, balance sheets, cash flow statements, and key financial metrics to assess the business's financial performance and viability. The financial projections help businesses evaluate their revenue potential, profitability, funding requirements, and return on investment. By developing realistic financial projections, businesses can demonstrate their financial health, attract investors, secure funding, and make informed decisions to drive sustainable growth and profitability.

A well-crafted business plan serves as a roadmap for entrepreneurs to navigate the complexities of the business landscape, articulate their vision, and achieve their strategic objectives. By outlining key components such as the executive summary, business description, market analysis, marketing and sales strategy, operations and management, and financial projections, businesses can develop a comprehensive and actionable plan to guide their operations, attract investors, and drive long-term success. A robust business plan not only helps businesses clarify their goals and strategies but also enables them to adapt to changing market conditions, seize opportunities, and overcome challenges to thrive in a competitive business environment.

Market Analysis and Strategy

The market analysis section of the business plan provides a comprehensive assessment of the industry landscape, target market segments, customer needs, and competitive dynamics. It includes market research findings, such as consumer trends, market size, growth opportunities, and competitive analysis, to inform the development of a robust marketing strategy and positioning plan. It also outlines the business's go-to-market strategy, pricing strategy, distribution channels, and sales tactics to effectively reach and engage target customers. The following is a hypothetical example on how a firm called Badume Tech undertook market analysis and strategy for its business.

Market Analysis and Strategy for Badume Tech:

1. Market Analysis:

Badume Tech is a technology startup specializing in innovative software solutions for small and medium-sized businesses (SMBs). The market analysis for Badume Tech identifies key trends, opportunities, and challenges in the SMB technology sector:

- Industry Landscape: The SMB technology sector is experiencing rapid growth, driven by increasing digitization, cloud adoption, and demand for scalable and cost-effective software solutions. With a focus on empowering SMBs with cutting-edge technology, Badume Tech is well-positioned to capitalize on this market trend.

- Market Trends: Key trends in the SMB technology market include the shift towards cloud-based solutions, the rise of mobile applications for business management, and the growing importance of data analytics and automation tools. Badume Tech aims to leverage these trends to develop innovative software products that address the evolving needs of SMBs.

Customer Needs: SMBs are seeking user-friendly, affordable, and customizable software solutions that can streamline their operations, enhance productivity, and drive growth. Badume Tech's market analysis highlights the importance of understanding and addressing these customer needs to create value-added products that resonate with the target market.

- Competitive Landscape: The SMB technology sector is highly competitive, with established players and new entrants vying for market share. Badume Tech's market analysis identifies key competitors, their strengths and weaknesses, and opportunities for differentiation. By offering unique features, superior customer support, and tailored solutions, Badume Tech aims to carve out a niche in the market and build a loyal customer base.

2. Marketing and Sales Strategy:

Based on the market analysis, Badume Tech has developed a comprehensive marketing and sales strategy to drive customer acquisition, retention, and revenue growth:

- Target Market: Badume Tech's target market includes small and medium-sized businesses across various industries, such as retail, hospitality, healthcare, and professional services. By segmenting the market based on industry, company size, and specific needs, Badume Tech can tailor its marketing messages and product offerings to different customer segments.

- Branding and Positioning: Badume Tech positions itself as a trusted partner for SMBs seeking innovative software solutions to streamline their operations and drive business growth. Through targeted branding initiatives, thought leadership content, and industry partnerships, Badume Tech aims to build brand awareness, credibility, and trust among its target audience.

- Marketing Channels: Badume Tech utilizes a mix of digital marketing channels, including social media, content marketing, email campaigns, and search engine optimization, to reach and engage with potential customers. By leveraging data analytics and marketing automation tools, Badume Tech can track customer interactions, measure campaign performance, and optimize marketing efforts for maximum impact.

- Sales Strategy: Badume Tech adopts a consultative sales approach, focusing on understanding customer needs, providing personalized solutions, and building long-term relationships. Through direct sales efforts, partnerships with resellers and channel partners, and online sales platforms, Badume Tech aims to drive sales growth, expand market reach, and maximize revenue opportunities.

In conclusion, Badume Tech's market analysis and strategy outline the company's market positioning, target market segments, competitive landscape, and marketing and sales initiatives to drive business growth and success in the SMB technology sector. By leveraging market insights, customer feedback, and industry trends, Badume Tech aims to develop innovative software solutions, build a strong brand presence, and create value for SMB customers, positioning itself as a leading provider of technology solutions for small and medium-sized businesses.

Significance of Applied Business Research to Entrepreneurs

Applied business research involves collecting, analyzing, and interpreting data to gain insights into business-related issues and trends. Applied business research plays a crucial role in empowering entrepreneurs to make informed decisions, drive strategic growth, and achieve long-term success in today's dynamic business environment. The significance of applied business research to entrepreneurs can be highlighted in the following ways:

1. Market Insights: Applied business research helps entrepreneurs gain valuable insights into market trends, customer preferences, competitive landscape, and industry dynamics. By conducting market research, entrepreneurs can identify emerging

opportunities, assess market demand, and develop innovative products or services that meet the needs of their target customers. This market intelligence enables entrepreneurs to make data-driven decisions, tailor their business strategies, and stay ahead of the competition.

2. Risk Mitigation: Entrepreneurs face various risks and uncertainties when launching or scaling their businesses. Applied business research allows entrepreneurs to assess risks, evaluate potential challenges, and develop risk mitigation strategies to safeguard their ventures. By conducting risk analysis, feasibility studies, and scenario planning, entrepreneurs can anticipate potential obstacles, identify vulnerabilities, and proactively address critical issues to minimize risks and optimize business outcomes.

3. Strategic Planning: Applied business research serves as a foundation for strategic planning and decision-making for entrepreneurs. By gathering and analyzing relevant data, entrepreneurs can assess market opportunities, set clear business objectives, and develop actionable strategies to achieve their goals. Whether it's entering new markets, launching new products, or expanding operations, applied business research provides entrepreneurs with the necessary insights and information to make strategic decisions that drive growth, improve competitiveness, and enhance overall business performance.

4. Customer Understanding: Understanding customer needs, preferences, and behaviors is essential for entrepreneurs to create value-added products, deliver exceptional customer experiences, and build brand loyalty. Applied business research enables entrepreneurs to gather customer feedback, conduct surveys, analyze consumer trends, and segment target markets to better

understand their customers. By leveraging customer insights, entrepreneurs can tailor their marketing strategies, improve product offerings, and enhance customer satisfaction, leading to increased sales, customer retention, and business growth.

5. Innovation and Differentiation: In today's competitive business landscape, innovation and differentiation are key drivers of success for entrepreneurs. Applied business research helps entrepreneurs identify market gaps, assess competitor strategies, and uncover opportunities for innovation and differentiation. By conducting product research, trend analysis, and competitive benchmarking, entrepreneurs can develop unique value propositions, differentiate their offerings, and position their businesses as industry leaders. This focus on innovation and differentiation enables entrepreneurs to stay relevant, attract customers, and sustain long-term growth in a competitive marketplace.

In conclusion, applied business research plays a pivotal role in empowering entrepreneurs to make strategic decisions, mitigate risks, understand their customers, drive innovation, and achieve sustainable growth in the ever-evolving business landscape. By leveraging the insights and knowledge gained from applied business research, entrepreneurs can enhance their decision-making processes, optimize business operations, and capitalize on opportunities to build successful and resilient businesses.

Data Collection and Analysis

Data collection and analysis are fundamental components of the research process that enable organizations to gather, organize, interpret, and derive meaningful insights from data to inform decision-making, solve problems, and drive business success. Here are key aspects of data collection and analysis:

1. Data Collection Methods:
    5. Surveys: Surveys involve collecting data from a sample of respondents through structured questionnaires or interviews. Surveys can be conducted online, over the phone, in-person, or through mail.
    6. Interviews: Interviews involve gathering data through one-on-one or group discussions with individuals to obtain in-depth insights, opinions, and perspectives.
    7. Observations: Observations involve collecting data by directly observing and recording behaviors, interactions, and events in real-time.
    8. Secondary Data: Secondary data refers to existing data sources, such as reports, articles, databases, and historical records, which can be analyzed to supplement primary data collection efforts.

2. Data Collection Tools:
    - Online Survey Platforms: Platforms like SurveyMonkey, Google Forms, and Qualtrics enable organizations to create and distribute surveys, collect responses, and analyze data.
    - Data Collection Apps: Mobile apps like SurveyCTO, Fulcrum, and Magpi allow organizations to collect data in the field, offline, and in real-time.
    - Data Analytics Software: Tools like SPSS, SAS, R, and Excel enable organizations to analyze and visualize data, perform statistical tests, and generate insights.

3. Data Analysis Techniques:
   - Descriptive Analysis: Descriptive analysis involves summarizing and presenting data through measures of central tendency, dispersion, frequency distributions, and graphical representations.
   - Inferential Analysis: Inferential analysis involves making inferences, predictions, and generalizations about a population based on sample data through statistical tests, hypothesis testing, and regression analysis.
   - Qualitative Analysis: Qualitative analysis involves analyzing textual or non-numeric data to identify themes, patterns, and meanings through techniques like content analysis, thematic analysis, and grounded theory.
   - Quantitative Analysis: Quantitative analysis involves analyzing numerical data to quantify relationships, trends, and patterns through statistical techniques like correlation analysis, regression analysis, and factor analysis.

4. Data Quality and Validity:
   - Data quality refers to the accuracy, completeness, consistency, and reliability of data collected, which impacts the validity and reliability of research findings.
   - Data validation techniques, such as data cleaning, data verification, and data validation checks, help ensure that collected data is accurate, consistent, and error-free.
   - Triangulation, which involves using multiple data sources, methods, or researchers to validate findings, enhances the credibility and trustworthiness of research results.

5. Data Visualization and Reporting:
   - Data visualization tools, such as charts, graphs, dashboards, and heat maps, help organizations visually represent and

communicate data insights in a clear, concise, and engaging manner.
- Data reports and summaries provide a structured overview of data collection methods, analysis techniques, findings, conclusions, and recommendations for stakeholders to make informed decisions.

In conclusion, effective data collection and analysis are essential for organizations to leverage data as a strategic asset, drive evidence-based decision-making, and gain competitive advantages in today's data-driven business landscape. By employing robust data collection methods, utilizing advanced data analysis techniques, ensuring data quality and validity, and presenting data insights through visualization and reporting, organizations can harness the power of data to drive innovation, optimize operations, and achieve organizational goals. Taking statistics and research method courses is essential for entrepreneurs lacking knowledge and skills in these areas.

Strategic Recommendations

Strategic recommendations are actionable insights and suggestions that organizations develop based on their analysis of internal and external factors to improve performance, achieve objectives, and gain a competitive advantage. Here are key considerations and best practices for formulating strategic recommendations:

1. SWOT Analysis:
   - Conduct a SWOT (Strengths, Weaknesses, Opportunities, Threats) analysis to identify internal strengths and weaknesses as well as external opportunities and threats facing the organization.

- Use the insights from the SWOT analysis to inform strategic recommendations that capitalize on strengths, address weaknesses, exploit opportunities, and mitigate threats.

2. Alignment with Business Goals:
   - Ensure that strategic recommendations are aligned with the organization's mission, vision, values, and strategic objectives.
   - Identify how each recommendation contributes to achieving specific business goals and objectives, whether they are related to growth, profitability, market share, customer satisfaction, or innovation.

3. Prioritization and Feasibility:
   - Prioritize strategic recommendations based on their potential impact, urgency, feasibility, and resource requirements.
   - Consider the organization's capabilities, constraints, and readiness to implement each recommendation effectively.

4. Innovation and Differentiation:
   - Include recommendations that focus on innovation, differentiation, and competitive positioning to create unique value propositions and stand out in the market.
   - Explore opportunities for product/service innovation, process optimization, technology adoption, and market expansion to drive growth and sustainability.

5. Risk Assessment and Mitigation:
   - Assess the risks associated with implementing each strategic recommendation, including financial, operational, competitive, regulatory, and reputational risks.
   - Develop risk mitigation strategies and contingency plans to address potential challenges and uncertainties that may arise during the implementation of recommendations.

6. Stakeholder Engagement:
   - Involve key stakeholders, including employees, customers, suppliers, investors, and partners, in the strategic recommendation process to gain diverse perspectives, insights, and *buy-in*. Buy-in refers to the process of obtaining support, agreement, or commitment from key stakeholders for a particular decision, initiative, or project. It involves actively involving stakeholders in the decision-making process, addressing their concerns, and ensuring that they understand and are aligned with the objectives and outcomes of the proposed action.

   - Communicate the rationale behind each recommendation, solicit feedback, address concerns, and build consensus to ensure successful implementation and adoption.

7. Monitoring and Evaluation:
   - Establish key performance indicators (KPIs) and metrics to track the progress, impact, and effectiveness of implementing strategic recommendations.
   - Regularly monitor and evaluate the outcomes, adjust strategies as needed, and learn from successes and failures to continuously improve organizational performance.

In conclusion, strategic recommendations serve as a roadmap for organizations to navigate challenges, seize opportunities, and achieve sustainable growth and success. By conducting thorough analysis, aligning recommendations with business goals, prioritizing initiatives, fostering innovation, managing risks, engaging stakeholders, and monitoring progress, organizations can develop and implement strategic recommendations that drive strategic change, enhance competitiveness, and create long-term value.

APPENDIX 1

GLOSSARY OF ENTREPRENUERSHIP AND INNOVATIONS TERMS

AI Algorithms: Mathematical algorithms used in artificial intelligence systems to process data and make decisions.

Angel Investors: Angel investors are affluent individuals who provide financial backing to startups in exchange for equity ownership. They often invest in early-stage companies and play a crucial role in supporting entrepreneurship by offering capital, mentorship, and industry connections.

Asset-based valuation: this is a valuation method that determines a company's value based on its tangible and intangible assets.

Balance sheet: a financial statement that provides a snapshot of a company's assets, liabilities, and shareholders' equity at a specific point in time.

Being proactive: Being proactive involves taking initiative, anticipating challenges, and acting in advance to prevent problems or capitalize on opportunities.

Being strategic: Being strategic involves setting long-term goals, making informed decisions, and aligning actions with the overall vision of the business.

Bootstrapping: this means self-funding. It involves using personal savings, credit cards, or assets to finance the business.

Breaking down silos: breaking down barriers or divisions between different departments or teams within an organization to encourage collaboration and communication.

Buy-in: the process of obtaining support, agreement, or commitment from key stakeholders for a particular decision, initiative, or project.

Cash flow: Cash flow represents the movement of money in and out of a business, indicating its liquidity and ability to meet financial obligations. Positive cash flow means that a company is generating more cash than it is spending, while negative cash flow may signal financial challenges.

Cash flow statement: a financial statement that shows the inflow and outflow of cash in a business over a specific period.

Chatbot: this is a computer program designed to simulate conversation with human users.

Cloud computing: the delivery of computing services over the internet, allowing users to access and store data and applications remotely.

Comparable company analysis: this is a valuation method that compares a company's financial metrics to those of similar publicly traded companies.

Competitive landscape: The competitive landscape refers to the overall market environment in which businesses operate, including competitors, industry trends, and market dynamics.

Corporate innovation: the process of developing and implementing new ideas, products, services, or business models within established organizations.

Crowdfunding: Crowdfunding is a method of raising capital from a large number of individuals, typically through online platforms, to finance a business venture or project. Entrepreneurs showcase their ideas to a broader audience, who can contribute varying amounts of money to support the initiative.

Cultural nuances: subtle or specific aspects of a culture that may affect communication, behavior, or decision-making.

Cultural intelligence: the ability to understand and navigate different cultural contexts effectively.

Customer Acquisition: Customer acquisition involves the process of attracting and converting potential customers into paying clients. Entrepreneurs employ various marketing, sales, and customer engagement strategies to acquire new customers, increase revenue, and grow their business.

Customer Lifetime Value: Customer Lifetime Value (CLV) is the predicted net profit a company expects to earn from a customer throughout their entire relationship with the business. Understanding CLV helps entrepreneurs assess the long-term value of customers, optimize marketing strategies, and prioritize customer retention efforts.

Customer pain points: customer pain points are specific problems, challenges, or frustrations that customers experience, which businesses aim to address and solve through their products or services.

Customer Segments: Customer segments are distinct groups of consumers with similar characteristics, needs, and behaviors. Entrepreneurs identify and target specific customer segments to tailor their products, marketing strategies, and customer experiences to meet the unique requirements of each group.

Customer-Centricity: Customer-centricity is a business approach that prioritizes delivering exceptional value and experiences to customers by understanding their needs, preferences, and feedback. Entrepreneurs who adopt a customer-centric mindset focus on building long-term relationships, driving loyalty, and creating sustainable growth.

Differentiated products or services: Differentiated products or services offer unique features, benefits, or qualities that set them apart from competitors in the market.

Digital-first economy: an economy where digital technologies and online channels play a central role in business operations and consumer interactions.

Discounted Cash Flow (DCF) Method: this is a valuation method used to estimate the value of an investment based on its projected future cash flows, discounted to present value.

Disruptive innovations: Disruptive innovations are groundbreaking advancements or technologies that create new markets, disrupt existing industries, and fundamentally change the way businesses operate.

Due diligence: the process of investigating and evaluating a company or investment before making a decision

ESG initiatives: Environmental, Social, and Governance initiatives that focus on sustainable and responsible business practices.

Feasibility Analysis: Feasibility analysis involves assessing the viability and potential success of a business idea or project based on factors such as market demand, resources, and technical feasibility.

Growth Trajectory: Growth trajectory refers to the path and rate at which a business expands over time. It involves analyzing factors such as revenue growth, market share, customer acquisition, and profitability to understand the trajectory of a company's growth and potential future performance.

Income statement: this is a financial statement that shows a company's revenues, expenses, and profits over a specific period.

Industry comparables: these are companies within the same industry that are used for comparison in financial analysis.

Initial public offering (IPO): this is the process by which a private company offers its shares to the public for the first time.

Iterating on the business model: Iterating on the business model involves making incremental changes and improvements to the core elements of a business model based on feedback and market insights.

Job Displacement: the loss of jobs due to automation, technology, or other factors.

Laggard: A laggard refers to an individual or organization that is slow to adopt new technologies, ideas, or trends compared to others in the market.

Leveraging Innovative Tactics: Leveraging innovative tactics involves using creative and unconventional approaches to solve problems, differentiate a business, and gain a competitive edge in the market. Entrepreneurs can leverage innovative tactics to drive growth, enhance customer engagement, and adapt to changing market conditions.

Mainstream adoption of a product: Mainstream adoption occurs when a product or service gains widespread acceptance and usage among the general population or target market.

Market Landscape: Market landscape refers to the overall structure, dynamics, and trends of a specific industry or market segment. Entrepreneurs analyze the market landscape to understand competitors, customer preferences, regulatory factors, and emerging opportunities that can influence their business strategy and decision-making.

Market Positioning: Market positioning involves defining how a company's products or services are perceived by customers relative to competitors. It encompasses strategies to differentiate a brand, target specific market segments, and create a unique value proposition to stand out in the marketplace.

Market Shifts: Market shifts refer to changes in consumer behavior, industry trends, technology advancements, or competitive dynamics that impact the business environment. Entrepreneurs need to monitor and respond to market shifts proactively to stay relevant, seize new opportunities, and mitigate risks.

Market validation: Market validation is the process of confirming the demand, viability, and potential success of a product or service through testing, research, and feedback from customers.

Monetization models: Monetization models outline how businesses generate revenue from their products or services, including pricing strategies, subscription models, and advertising methods.

Natural Language Processing (NLP): a branch of AI that enables computers to understand, interpret, and generate human language.

Payables: amounts owed by a company to suppliers or vendors for goods or services received on credit.

Precedent transactions analysis: this is a valuation method that uses the prices paid in past M&A transactions involving similar companies to estimate the value of a target company.

Product Development: Product development is the process of creating, designing, and bringing new products or services to market. It involves research, ideation, prototyping, testing, and refinement to ensure that the product meets customer needs and aligns with the company's objectives.

Product-Market Fit: Product-Market Fit refers to the alignment between a company's product or service offering and the needs and preferences of its target market. Achieving product-market fit indicates that the product resonates with customers, solves a significant problem, and generates strong demand in the market.

Prototype: A prototype is a preliminary version or model of a product or service used to test and validate ideas, gather feedback, and make improvements before full-scale production.

Prototyping ideas: Prototyping ideas involves creating tangible representations or mock-ups of concepts to visualize, test, and refine new product or service ideas.

Ratio analysis: this refers to the process of analyzing and interpreting financial ratios to evaluate a company's performance and financial health.

Receivables: amounts owed to a company by customers for goods or services provided on credit.
Red flags: warning signs or indicators of potential problems or risks in a business or investment.

Revenue Model: A revenue model outlines how a business generates income through sales, subscriptions, advertising, or other revenue streams.

Robotic process automation: the use of software robots or bots to automate repetitive tasks and processes.

Scalable business models: Scalable business models are designed to grow and expand efficiently without compromising quality or increasing costs exponentially as the business expands.

Sentiment analysis: the process of analyzing text to determine the sentiment or emotion expressed, often used in social media monitoring and customer feedback analysis.

Staying ahead of the curve: Staying ahead of the curve involves anticipating trends, innovations, and market shifts to maintain a competitive edge and lead the industry.

Streamlining Processes: Streamlining processes involves optimizing and simplifying the workflows, procedures, and operations within a business to improve efficiency, reduce costs, and enhance productivity. Entrepreneurs streamline processes to eliminate bottlenecks, minimize waste, and deliver products or services more effectively to customers.

Supply Chain Disruptions: Supply chain disruptions occur when there are interruptions or challenges in the flow of goods, materials, or information within a company's supply chain. These disruptions can be caused by factors such as natural disasters, geopolitical issues, or unexpected events, impacting a business's operations and ability to meet customer demand.

SWOT Analysis: SWOT analysis is a strategic planning tool used to assess a company's Strengths, Weaknesses, Opportunities, and Threats. By identifying these internal and external factors, entrepreneurs can make informed decisions, capitalize on strengths, address weaknesses, seize opportunities, and mitigate risks.

Think outside the box: Thinking outside the box means approaching problems or situations in unconventional or innovative ways to find creative solutions.

Value drivers: factors that significantly impact the value of a business or investment.

Value Proposition: A value proposition is a statement that communicates the unique benefits and value that a product or service offers to customers.

Variance analysis: this is a technique used to compare actual financial performance against planned or budgeted performance to identify differences and analyze their causes.

Venture Capital: Venture capital is a type of private equity investment provided to early-stage, high-potential startups with the expectation of significant returns. Venture capitalists typically take equity stakes in companies and provide funding, expertise, and support to help them grow and succeed.

Virtual assistant: this is an AI-powered software program that can assist users with tasks such as scheduling, reminders, and information retrieval.

Virtual collaboration tools: software and platforms that enable remote teams to collaborate and communicate effectively.

APPENDIX II
SAMPLE BUSINESS PLAN

BUSINESS PLAN FOR SALIM SOCIAL VENTURES

PREPARED BY AHMAD SALIM

1. EXECUTIVE SUMMARY

Ahmad Salim, inspired by insights from the MBA digest course on Entrepreneurship and Innovation, particularly the Bird-in-Hand Principle and the Crazy Quilt Principle of Saras Sarasvathy's effectuation theory, embarked on a journey to establish Salim Social Ventures. The Bird-in-Hand Principle, advocating for entrepreneurs to leverage their existing resources such as skills, knowledge, and network, guided Ahmad in laying the foundation for Salim Social Ventures. Embracing the Crazy Quilt Principle, which underscores the value of forging partnerships and alliances to co-create value and share resources, Ahmad strategically positioned this company for growth and sustainability.

Conducting thorough internet-based research, Ahmad identified a promising entrepreneurial opportunity in roselle processing and trade. Moreover, he grasped the significance and relevance of transforming his business into a social enterprise, blending the mission-driven ethos of non-profit organizations with the revenue-generating model of for-profit businesses.

Mission Statement:

"At Salim Social Ventures, our mission is to empower local farmers, provide employment opportunities and deliver high-quality roselle products to consumers. We are committed to creating a ripple effect that extends beyond profits."

Vision Statement:

"Our vision at Salim Social Ventures is to be a leading force in the roselle industry, known for our ethical sourcing practices, innovative products, and positive contribution to society."

Salim Social Ventures is strategically located in Tumfafi village, near Dawanau Market, a bustling hub of economic activity. It will have a production facility equipped with machinery for processing and packaging roselle products. Its key objectives include the following:

1. Establish sustainable farming practices to ensure a stable and quality supply of roselle.

2. Develop innovative roselle-based products that cater to health-conscious consumers.

3. Expand distribution channels to reach a wider market and increase brand visibility.

4. Foster community engagement through educational initiatives on the benefits of roselle and sustainable living practices.

Our target market includes health-conscious individuals, herbal tea enthusiasts, and consumers looking for natural and unique beverage options. We aim to attract a diverse customer base spanning across different age groups, with a focus on urban areas where there is a growing demand for organic and sustainable products. Our marketing tactics will include utilizing social media platforms like Instagram, Facebook, and Twitter to engage with customers, share product information, and showcase the health benefits of roselle.

Competitive Advantages:

1. Sustainable Sourcing: We work directly with local farmers, ensuring fair compensation and environmentally friendly farming methods.

2. Product Innovation: Our focus on developing innovative roselle-based products sets us apart in the market. From unique herbal teas to healthy snacks and beauty products, we continuously

strive to create new and exciting offerings that cater to the diverse needs and preferences of our target market.

3. Market Responsiveness: We are agile and responsive to consumer trends and preferences, allowing us to quickly adapt our product offerings and marketing strategies to meet evolving market demands.

Funding and Financial Projections:

We are seeking contributions to our crowdfunding campaign to achieve a funding goal of N20,000,000. Your support will enable us to drive our mission forward and create a positive impact in the roselle industry and local communities.

Key financial projections include: Year 1 Revenue: N10,000,000, Year 2 Revenue: N15,000,000 Year 3 Revenue: N20,000,000; and the 2027 balance sheet with Assets: ₦6,000,000, Liabilities: ₦1,000,000 and Equity: ₦5,000,000.

2. BUSINESS DESCRIPTION

Salim Social Ventures, founded by the enterprising youth Ahmad Salim, is a dynamic firm at the forefront of the dried hibiscus leaves trade in Nigeria. With a rich background in sourcing quality roselle from Kano, Jigawa, and Katsina states, Ahmad leverages his three years of industry experience to deliver top-notch products to clients.

Despite facing challenges in the job market after graduating with a degree in sociology, Ahmad's entrepreneurial spirit led him to establish his business in 2021. His initial success supplying a merchant in Dawanau Market, Kano, laid the foundation for what would become Salim Social Ventures. In 2022, the firm was officially registered with the Corporate Affairs Commission, marking a significant milestone in Ahmad's journey.

Driven by a thirst for knowledge and growth, Ahmad enrolled in an MBA digest course on Entrepreneurship and Innovation, offered on the Udemy platform. Completing the course in just 12 weeks, he honed his entrepreneurial skills and gained valuable insights to propel his business forward. Armed with a deep understanding of the market, a strong network of farmers and traders, and expertise in social mobilization, Ahmad is poised to elevate Salim Social Ventures to new heights of success.

Salim Social Ventures operates at the heart of the bustling Dawanau Market, where the meticulous process of cleaning, processing, packaging, and exporting roselle takes place. Only the finest dried hibiscus leaves are selected for further processing.

The roselle undergoes a thorough cleaning process to remove impurities and ensure hygiene standards are met. Skilled workers then handle the delicate processing phase, where the leaves are carefully dried and prepared for packaging. Utilizing modern equipment and techniques guarantees that the roselle retains its freshness and nutritional value throughout the process.

Packaging is a critical step in the export chain. With a focus on expanding into international markets, Salim Social Ventures is committed to maintaining the highest quality standards in every aspect of the roselle supply chain, this requires sufficient funding which company lacks presently.

3. MARKET ANALYSIS

Salim Social Ventures operates in the thriving dried hibiscus leaves industry in Nigeria, with a focus on sourcing, processing, packaging, and exporting roselle from Kano, Jigawa, and Katsina states. The industry landscape is characterized by a growing demand for natural and healthy products both domestically and internationally. With consumers increasingly seeking organic and ethically sourced ingredients, the market for roselle presents significant opportunities for growth and innovation.

Market Trends:

- Increasing consumer awareness of the health benefits of roselle, such as its high antioxidant content and potential medicinal properties.

- Growing interest in sustainable and environmentally friendly agricultural practices, driving demand for ethically sourced roselle products.

- Rising popularity of herbal teas and natural beverages, with roselle being a key ingredient in many traditional and modern recipes.

- Expansion of international trade networks, offering opportunities for Salim Social Ventures to access new markets and increase export volumes.

Customer Needs:

- Customers in both domestic and international markets seek high-quality roselle products that are clean, fresh, and free from contaminants.

- There is a demand for convenient and attractively packaged roselle products that meet international food safety standards.

- Customers value transparency in the sourcing and processing of roselle, with a preference for products that support local farmers and communities.

- Health-conscious consumers are looking for natural alternatives to processed beverages, making roselle a popular choice for its nutritional benefits.

Competitive Forces:

- Salim Social Ventures faces competition from other suppliers and exporters of roselle in Nigeria, each vying for market share based on product quality, pricing, and customer service.

- The company must navigate competitive forces in the global market, including fluctuating commodity prices, trade regulations, and the emergence of new competitors in the industry.

- Building strong relationships with customers, maintaining consistent product quality, and offering competitive pricing will be key factors in staying ahead of competitors.

Target Market Segments:

- Salim Social Ventures targets health-conscious consumers who prioritize natural ingredients and seek out products with proven health benefits.

- The company also caters to international buyers looking for premium roselle products sourced from reputable suppliers with a track record of excellence.

- With a focus on ethical sourcing and sustainable practices, Salim Social Ventures appeals to customers who value transparency and social responsibility in their purchasing decisions.

- The target market includes retailers, wholesalers, herbal tea manufacturers, and health food stores both in Nigeria and abroad, seeking reliable and high-quality roselle products for their businesses.

In conclusion, Salim Social Ventures is well-positioned to capitalize on the growing demand for roselle products by offering premium quality, ethically sourced, and competitively priced offerings that cater to the evolving needs of customers in Nigeria and beyond.

4. MARKETING AND SALES STRATEGY

Salim Social Ventures will deploy a multifaceted marketing and sales strategy to effectively promote its premium roselle products, attract customers, and drive revenue growth. The strategy will encompass a mix of traditional and digital marketing tactics, strategic sales channels, competitive pricing strategies, branding initiatives, and customer acquisition plans.

Marketing Tactics:

- Utilize social media platforms like Instagram, Facebook, and Twitter to engage with customers, share product information, and showcase the health benefits of roselle.

- Implement targeted digital advertising campaigns to reach health-conscious consumers, herbal tea manufacturers, and retailers interested in natural ingredients.

- Collaborate with influencers and health bloggers to create buzz around Salim Social Ventures' roselle products and attract a wider audience.

- Develop a content marketing strategy that includes blog posts, videos, and infographics highlighting the uses and benefits of roselle in various culinary and wellness applications.

Sales Channels:

- Establish an e-commerce platform on the company website to enable direct sales to consumers, offering convenient online purchasing and delivery options.

- Forge partnerships with local retailers, health food stores, and specialty tea shops to distribute Salim Social Ventures' roselle products in key markets.

- Explore opportunities for wholesale distribution to restaurants, cafes, and health-focused establishments looking to incorporate roselle into their menus.

- Consider participation in farmers' markets, food festivals, and pop-up events to showcase products, engage with customers, and drive sales through in-person interactions.

Pricing Strategies:

- Implement a dynamic pricing strategy that balances the premium quality of Salim Social Ventures' roselle products with competitive pricing to appeal to target customers.

- Offer promotional discounts, bundle deals, and seasonal offers to incentivize purchases and drive customer loyalty.

- Conduct regular pricing analysis to stay competitive in the market, adjust pricing strategies based on market trends, and maximize revenue opportunities.

Branding Initiatives:

- Develop a compelling brand identity that conveys Salim Social Ventures' commitment to quality, sustainability, and social impact, resonating with eco-conscious and health-focused consumers.

- Design visually appealing packaging that reflects the freshness and natural goodness of roselle, standing out on shelves and attracting attention from potential customers.

- Establish brand consistency across all touchpoints, including website, social media, packaging, and marketing materials, to build brand recognition and trust among consumers.

Customer Acquisition Plans:

- Offer product samples, trial packs, and exclusive promotions to encourage first-time purchases and introduce customers to the unique flavors and benefits of Salim Social Ventures' roselle products.

- Implement a customer loyalty program that rewards repeat purchases, referrals, and reviews to foster long-term relationships and drive customer retention.

- Collect and analyze customer feedback to continuously improve products, services, and customer experiences, demonstrating a commitment to customer satisfaction and product excellence.

In summary, Salim Social Ventures' marketing and sales strategy is designed to create brand awareness, attract a loyal customer base, and generate revenue by leveraging a mix of marketing tactics, strategic sales channels, competitive pricing strategies, strong branding initiatives, and customer-centric acquisition plans. By focusing on quality, innovation, and customer engagement, the company aims to establish itself as a leading provider of premium roselle products in the market.

5. OPERATIONS AND MANAGEMENT

Organizational Structure:

Salim Social Ventures will operate under a functional organizational structure, with key departments including operations, marketing, finance, and production. The key roles within the company are as follows:

- Founder/CEO (Salim): Responsible for setting the strategic direction of the company, overseeing business development, and managing stakeholder relationships.

- Operations Manager: Manages day-to-day operations, production processes, and supply chain logistics.

- Marketing Manager: Leads marketing campaigns, brand development, and customer engagement strategies.

- Finance Manager: Handles financial planning, budgeting, and reporting functions.

-Production Supervisor: Oversees manufacturing processes, quality control, and inventory management.

Key Personnel:

- Ahmad Salim: Visionary leader with a passion for sustainable agriculture and social entrepreneurship.

- Operations Manager: Experienced professional with a background in operations management and process optimization.

- Marketing Manager: Creative individual with expertise in digital marketing and brand building.

- Finance Manager: Seasoned finance professional responsible for financial strategy and performance monitoring.

- Production Supervisor: Skilled individual with knowledge of production processes and quality assurance.

Operational Processes:

- Salim Social Ventures will implement efficient operational processes to ensure smooth production and delivery of roselle products.

- The company will establish clear SOPs for each operational task to maintain consistency and quality standards.

- Regular quality control checks will be conducted to ensure that products meet regulatory requirements and customer expectations.

- Continuous improvement initiatives will be implemented to enhance operational efficiency and productivity.

Production Capabilities:

- Salim Social Ventures will have a production facility equipped with machinery for processing and packaging roselle products.

- The production team will have the capability to produce a variety of roselle-based products, such as teas, jams, and dried flowers.

- Sustainable practices will be integrated into production processes to minimize waste and environmental impact.

Resource Requirements:

- Human Resources: Skilled production staff, sales representatives, and administrative personnel to support daily operations.

- Financial Resources: Capital for equipment acquisition, raw material procurement, marketing activities, and operational expenses.

- Physical Resources: Production facility, storage space, 3 laptops, packaging materials, and transportation vehicles.

Management Approach:

- Salim Social Ventures will adopt a collaborative management approach, fostering open communication, teamwork, and a shared commitment to the company's goals.

- Decision-making will be inclusive, with input from team members across departments to leverage diverse perspectives and expertise.

- Regular performance evaluations and feedback sessions will be conducted to monitor progress, address challenges, and set goals for improvement.

Operational Workflows and Systems:

- The company will implement an ERP system to streamline operational workflows, manage inventory, and track production processes. ERP stands for Enterprise Resource Planning. It is a type of software system that integrates various business functions and processes into a unified platform. ERP systems are designed to streamline operations, improve efficiency, and provide real-time insights for decision-making within an organization.

- Standard operating procedures (SOPs) will be developed for key operational tasks to ensure consistency and efficiency.

- A culture of innovation and continuous learning will be promoted, encouraging team members to propose and implement process improvements and operational efficiencies.

In conclusion, Salim Social Ventures' operations and management strategy is designed to ensure effective leadership, streamlined processes, optimal production capabilities, and resource management. By fostering collaboration, innovation, and operational excellence, the company aims to deliver high-quality roselle products, drive growth, and create value for customers and stakeholders.

6. FINANCIAL PROJECTIONS

Funding:

- Salim Social Ventures aims to raise ₦20,000,000 through crowdfunding to provide employment opportunities to youth, support growth initiatives and operational expenses over the next three years (2025-2027.

Budget Estimates:

- Operating Expenses:

  - 2025: ₦5,000,000

- 2026: ₦6,000,000

  - 2027: ₦7,000,000

- Marketing and Advertising:

  - 2025: ₦2,000,000

  - 2026: ₦2,500,000

  - 2027: ₦3,000,000

- Research and Development:

  - 2025: ₦1,500,000

  - 2026: ₦1,800,000

  - 2027: ₦2,200,000

- Administrative Costs:

  - 2025: ₦1,000,000

  - 2026: ₦1,200,000

  - 2027: ₦1,500,000

Revenue Projections:

- 2025: ₦10,000,000

- 2026: ₦15,000,000

- 2027: ₦20,000,000

Income Statement (2025-2027):

2025:

  - Revenue: ₦10,000,000

  - Cost of Goods Sold: ₦3,000,000

  - Gross Profit: ₦7,000,000

  - Operating Expenses: ₦5,000,000

  - Net Profit: ₦2,000,000

2026:

  - Revenue: ₦15,000,000

  - Cost of Goods Sold: ₦4,500,000

  - Gross Profit: ₦10,500,000

  - Operating Expenses: ₦6,000,000

  - Net Profit: ₦4,500,000

2027:

- Revenue: ₦20,000,000

- Cost of Goods Sold: ₦6,000,000

- Gross Profit: ₦14,000,000

- Operating Expenses: ₦7,000,000

- Net Profit: ₦7,000,000

Balance Sheet (2025-2027):

2025:

- Assets: ₦3,000,000

- Liabilities: ₦500,000

- Equity: ₦2,500,000

2026:

- Assets: ₦4,500,000

- Liabilities: ₦800,000

- Equity: ₦3,700,000

2027:

  - Assets: ₦6,000,000

  - Liabilities: ₦1,000,000

  - Equity: ₦5,000,000

Cash Flow Statement (2025-2027):

2025:

  - Operating Cash Flow: ₦5,000,000

  - Investing Cash Flow: -₦1,500,000

  - Financing Cash Flow: -₦1,000,000

2026:

  - Operating Cash Flow: ₦8,000,000

  - Investing Cash Flow: -₦2,000,000

  - Financing Cash Flow: -₦1,500,000

2027:

  - Operating Cash Flow: ₦10,000,000

- Investing Cash Flow: -₦3,000,000

- Financing Cash Flow: -₦2,000,000

These Balance Sheet and Cash Flow Statement details cover the years 2025, 2026, and 2027 for Salim Social Ventures. The Balance Sheet shows the company's assets, liabilities, and equity for each year, while the Cash Flow Statement outlines the operating, investing, and financing cash flows over the same period.

Key Financial Metrics (2025-2027):

2025:

- Gross Margin: 65%

- Net Profit Margin: 20%

- Return on Investment (ROI): 40%

2026:

- Gross Margin: 68%

- Net Profit Margin: 25%

- Return on Investment (ROI): 45%

2027:

- Gross Margin: 70%

- Net Profit Margin: 30%

- Return on Investment (ROI): 50%

Notes: Explanation of Financial Terms

1. Cost of Goods Sold (COGS:

Cost of Goods Sold represents the direct costs associated with producing the goods sold by the company. It includes expenses such as raw materials, labor, and manufacturing overhead. COGS is subtracted from revenue to calculate Gross Profit.

2. Gross Profit:

Gross Profit is the difference between revenue and the cost of goods sold. It reflects how efficiently a company is producing and selling its products. A higher gross profit margin indicates better profitability.

3. Net Profit:

Net Profit is the amount of revenue that remains after deducting all expenses, including COGS and operating expenses. It is a key indicator of a company's overall profitability.

4. Operating Expenses:

Operating Expenses are the costs incurred in the day-to-day operations of a business. This includes expenses such as salaries, rent, utilities, marketing, and administrative costs.

5. Operating Cash Flow:

Operating Cash Flow is the cash generated or used by a company's core business operations. It helps assess a company's ability to generate cash from its regular business activities.

6. Investing Cash Flow:

Investing Cash Flow represents the cash flow from investments in assets such as equipment, property, or securities. It reflects the company's capital expenditures and acquisitions.

7. Financing Cash Flow:

Financing Cash Flow includes cash flow from activities related to raising capital or repaying debt. It shows how a company is financing its operations and growth.

8. Gross Margin:

Gross Margin is a financial metric that indicates the percentage of revenue that exceeds the cost of goods sold. It is calculated as (Revenue - COGS) / Revenue and is a measure of a company's profitability.

9. Net Profit Margin:

Net Profit Margin is a profitability ratio that shows the percentage of revenue that translates into net profit. It is calculated as Net Profit / Revenue and measures how well a company is managing its expenses relative to revenue.

10. Return on Investment (ROI):

Return on Investment is a financial metric that evaluates the profitability of an investment. It is calculated as (Net Profit / Investment Cost) x 100 and helps investors assess the efficiency of their investments.

11. Equity

In the context of Salim Social Ventures, equity represents the ownership interest in the company held by its shareholders (Salim and four other people). It represents the funds contributed by the owners and retained earnings over time.

www.ingramcontent.com/pod-product-compliance
Lightning Source LLC
Chambersburg PA
CBHW052255220526
45471CB00001B/349